A TRIBUTE

TO THE

PRINCIPLES, VIRTUES, HABITS AND PUBLIC USEFULNESS

OF THE

Irish and Scotch Early Settlers

OF PENNSYLVANIA.

BY A DESCENDANT.

CHAMBERSBURG, PA.:
PRINTED BY M. KIEFFER & CO.
1856.

PREFACE.

THE writer of the Tribute contained in this work, had long desired to see from the Historical publications in Pennsylvania, a vindication of the character and principles of the Irish and Scotch early settlers of this great State and their descendants against reproach, as well as aspersion, cast upon them in some modern compilations having pretensions to Historical accuracy.

Appreciating highly the religious and moral character, intelligence, industry and energy of those settlers, as well as their great usefulness in raising the standard of education—in promoting religious Christian influence—in defending the frontier against the wars of the French and Indians, and in their patriotic devotion of their lives and fortunes to the cause of American Independence; he did think if there were any class of citizens of Pennsylvania entitled to gratitude and reverence, not only from their descendants, but from all others enjoying the blessings of a home and residence under this free government, it was the Irish and Scotch early settlers of Pennsylvania.

The events in the lives of these men, and the incidents of the times in which they were actors, political, civil, religious or military, which led to the prosperity of the State and the establishment of the free institutions under which we live, prosper and are happy, should be to every American citizen objects of peculiar interest.

Instead of acknowledgments of gratitude and reverence for the men who were the pioneers of the Province of Pennsylvania, laying broad and deep the foundations of its prosperity and republican government, we have been chagrined to find them slighted in some historical compilations of Pennsylvania History; whilst by others, we have been incensed at the unjust and unfounded aspersions cast upon the race.

Having the blood of some of those early settlers flowing in our veins, and having been born, ever lived and prospered on Pennsylvania soil, we feel as if we were under obligations, in common with many others, to come up to the vindication of the reputation of ancestors, who long since have rested from their labors, and who, by toil and sacrifices, did much to achieve the inheritance which their posterity and others are enjoying.

We have presumed to offer the sketch herein contained as our Tribute to the memory and reverence of those settlers. The writer, feeling as if the sand of his Time glass was nearly run out, and that he ere long must be laid aside from labor, and that if any thing were done by him in vindication of the principles, virtues and habits, of these settlers of a past age, it must be done quickly—has hastily thrown together in his leisure hours, taken from other avocations, the remarks contained in the subsequent pages.

It has little merit, other than a compilation from public documents, historical records, and traditions from reliable sources, together with some observations of the writer, whose reminiscences go into the past century.

It is but a summary of facts and illustrations and an outline to be extended by some one better qualified, having more time and better access to historical collections of the early history of Pennsylvania, of which there is a dearth. It will be ample gratification to him if this Tribute shall be a leader to some more extended vindication of the character of the Irish and Scotch early settlers of Pennsylvania, which will be worthy of a place amongst the historical records of this great State.

The author acknowledges his obligations for information, in the preparation of this work, to Dr. Foote's Sketches of North Carolina—and Virginia—Day's Historical collections—Dr. Smith's Old Redstone—Dr. Alexander's Log College—Dr. Miller's Life of Dr. Rogers—Dr. Elliott's Life of McCurdy and others—Craig's History of Pittsburg—Hazard's Colonial Records and Archives of Pennsylvania, and American Archives by Force—and Gordon's History of Pennsylvania—Mr. Rupp's—Histories of Lancaster, Cumberland and Franklin counties.

Chambersburg, Pa. G. C.

CHAPTER I.

Classes of Emigrants—Dissensions—Rivalries—James Logan —Dickinson—Franklin in opposition to Emigrants—Mr. Day's accusation—Trespasses on Lands claimed by Indians —Their complaints—Redress—Other causes of dissatisfaction with the white Inhabitants and Proprietory Agents—Traders—and French Influence—Causes of War.

THE Province of Pennsylvania was early attractive to emigrants from other countries. It was recommended by its free and constitutional government—by the character of its fundamental Laws, adopted and established by the first emigrants to its territory—its fertile soil, salubrious and temperate climate —its adaptation to a large and rural population; with advantages for trade, commerce and manufactures. The dissatisfaction prevailing with large classes of intelligent, industrious and enterprising men, under several of the European governments, directed their attention to the American colonies, and to men of this character, Pennsylvania was generally preferred for their abode, after the organization of its government.

The population of Pennsylvania was made up of emigrants from various parts of Europe. They were not homogeneous, but were diversified by their origin, religious principles, habits, and language. They were united in devotion to the principles of the Reformation, and in favor of civil and religious liberty. Equality of rights and the liberty of worship according to the dictates of conscience, were standard principles so founded and guarded, that no party or power dared to assail them. These established and avowed principles made Pennsylvania a desirable asylum for the oppressed and persecuted of all nations.

The diversity which characterized the inhabitants, divided them into three classes, whose separation was maintained unbroken for some generations, and is not even yet effaced. They were the English, the Scots and Irish, and the Germans. The associates and followers of Penn, who were amongst the first to establish her government, were an honest, intelligent, virtuous, peaceful and benevolent population, known in England and the Colonies by the name of Friends or Quakers. Much of the wealth of the Province was with them, and as their location was in the city of Philadelphia, or in the country near it, they were influential in the organization of the Provincial government. They were able also, from their numbers, to maintain an ascendency in the Assembly, and control its legislation. As the Proprietory was, in his associations and principles, of their Society, there was generally harmony and correspondent sentiment between the Quaker party and the Proprietory and the officers of his appointment, most of whom were of the Society of Friends. The Quakers were an orderly, industrious and law abiding people, cultivating peace with all men. They had their peculiarities of dress, manners, language and religious worship, opposition to war and military service, which distinguished them from the other population of the Province.

The Germans were of different denominations of Christians and various origin. The Swiss Mennonites were amongst the earliest who entered this Province, about the beginning of the last century. They came in considerable numbers and settled in the neighborhood of Philadelphia, about Pequea and other parts of what formed Lancaster county. They were orderly, industrious and frugal, farmers; peaceful and honest in all their relations and dealings. They resembled the Quakers in opposition to war and military service, and in maintenance of peace principles. The Lutheran and German Reformed Germans, who had been emigrating since 1710, settled before 1720 in considerable numbers in parts of what are now in the counties of Montgomery, Bucks, Berks and Lancaster. Others of the same class continued to arrive yearly, and in some years the influx of these German emigrants was so great as to alarm some of the English first settlers, lest the Germans should make a German province of Pennsylvania. Amongst these Germans, though mostly Lutheran and German Reformed, there were some Mennonites and Dunkards.

The French Huguenots who settled in Pennsylvania were but few, some of whom settled about 1712 on Pequea creek, which seems to have been an attractive country for settlement to emigrants from different parts of Europe.

These Germans were a hardy, frugal and industrious people, and in many districts have preserved their foreign manners and language. They have established in every part of the State, communities much respected for religious and moral character; many of them emigrated for conscience' sake, and others to improve their condition and circumstances. Their industry and frugality have enabled them to add greatly to their own wealth and resources, whilst they were increasing that of the Province and State. With most of this class, education has been promoted and their descendants, in acquirements and intelligence, are in advance of their ancestors, and many are amongst the most respectable and useful citizens of the Commonwealth, whilst they have, by branches of their families, contributed greatly to the industrious and useful population of several of the Western States.

Emigrants from Scotland and Ireland constituted a large portion of the early settlers of Pennsylvania. Many of these were called Scotch-Irish, from the circumstance that they were the descendants of Scots, who had by the government been encouraged to take up their residence in the north of Ireland, and to the improvement and civilization of which they had greatly contributed; but being oppressed by the tyranny and exactions of a despotic and profligate monarch, and the restrictions and penalties imposed by an obsequious parliament, as well as the intolerance and persecutions of a haughty hierarchy, expatriated themselves, with their families to the American colonies. To these were added many of the native Irish from the north of Ireland, as well as emigrants from Scotland. Pennsylvania was the selection of most of them, when they considered, that, under the charter of Penn and the fundamental laws of the Province, they could enjoy civil and religious liberty. They sought an asylum from Church and State intolerance and oppression, if it were to be had only in the wilderness of another continent, under a government of equal rights. They were nearly all Presbyterians in their Church relations, and many of them had settled in Pennsylvania before the close of the seventeenth century.

The emigrants from Ireland and Scotland approached so close in national character, and were so congenial in sentiments, habits and religious principles, having in the land from which they emigrated, suffered from common grievances, that they were identified as one people. As professors of religion, they united in church organizations and worshipped together at the same Christian altars.

The first settlements of this class were in Bucks county, but chiefly in the territory, which, in 1729, was organized into the county of Lancaster. Settlements were made in it about 1717, on Octorora creek, and about the same time or earlier, in Pequea, and in 1722 in Donegal and Paxton. In 1730 and '34, the same class of emigrants, with the license of the Proprietory government, located themselves in the Kittochtinny valley, west of the Susquehanna, where they increased rapidly and in a few years formed there a large, respectable and influential community.

Under a free government of equal rights, with political power accessible to all the citizens, it was to be expected that amongst these different classes or races of emigrants, there would be rivalries and competition, as well as jealousies of ascendency and political power. They would be apt to differ in their opinions of public measures, as well as in their predilections for the men who were to establish measures or execute them.

The Quakers had the advantage of the other classes, that they were parties to the first organization of the government, and in the establishment of the three first counties of Philadelphia, Chester and Bucks, and in regulating their representation. In those counties they had the majority of the inhabitants, which enabled them to elect as members of Assembly and Council, such as were entirely acceptable to them.

Their majority in the Assembly, which prevailed for a long time, made its legislation to conform to their wishes and principles ; the Proprietory, who belonged to their Society, being disposed generally to coöperate with them.

From the great influx of emigrants from Ireland, Scotland and Germany, there was every prospect, that the control of the

Legislature of the provincial government would pass from the hands of the Quakers into that of one of these other classes, and that they, who had been instrumental in establishing the government and putting it in operation, should be reduced to a powerless minority.

In the early administration of the Provincial government, James Logan was a prominent, intelligent and influential member, being for many years a member of Council, and also the President of Council, as well as enjoying other high and important offices. Though of Irish origin, he had become affiliated with the Society of Friends, of which he professed to be one. He adopted their principles and manifested his willingness to maintain them, except he was disposed to go further for the defence of the country against its enemies, and was not entirely adverse to all military measures.

He had, however, the confidence of the Quaker party, who retained him in influential stations of the government, as long as his health and age would allow. Logan saw clearly, from the accession which the Province was yearly receiving of substantial, intelligent and respectable emigrants from Scotland and Ireland, that the Quaker rule in the government would be restrained or supplanted. He knew well the character of his countrymen, to be inquisitive, energetic, and independent. They would know their rights, and knowing them, would dare to maintain them without the fear of man. It was not to be expected that men, who had scrutinized and contested the powers of a royal government, were going to live passive under the administration of a government in which they had equal rights with all its citizens. The day must come, when their voice would be heard, felt and respected in the government of the Province.

They did exercise their right of suffrage at the elections in Lancaster and York counties, in opposition to the candidate selected from and supported by the Quakers. They were sometimes successful in their opposition, and in the election of their own candidates. In these election contests there was much excitement and feeling, and they were attended with irregularities, disorder and breaches of the peace discreditable to the authors; yet, these excesses were short of like disorders and of the frauds committed on the elective franchise, in these days of progress and refinement, under the laws of our great Republic, and which are to be reprobated as great public offences, subversive of the rights of the citizens and the purity of elections, and reproachful to the law and its officers. In these election contests the Germans generally took part with the Friends and supported their candidates. The German Mennonites accorded so much with the Quakers, in their opposition to military service, supplies or measures of defence, that they were the partisans of the candidate supported by the Quakers. About this time James Logan began to undervalue his countrymen, and speak disparagingly of emigrants from Ireland, as being undesirable settlers.

In 1729 he expresses "himself glad to find that the Parliament is about to take measures to prevent their too free emigration to this country." "It looks," says he, "as if Ireland is to send all her inhabitants hither; for last week not less than six ships arrived, and every day two or three arrive also. The common fear is, that if they continue to come, they will make themselves proprietors of the province." "It is strange," says he, "that they thus crowd where they are not wanted." What made him pronounce them "audacious and disorderly," was, that they entered on and settled lands in the southern part of Lancaster county, towards the Maryland line, "York Barrens," without approaching him to propose to purchase, and when challenged for their titles, said, as their excuse, "that the Proprietory and his agents had solicited for colonists and that they had come accordingly."

And in 1725 he complains "that there are so much as one hundred thousand acres of land possessed by persons (including Germans), who resolutely set down and improve lands, without any right, and he is much at a loss to determine how to dispossess them."

He also represents the Irish emigrants as "troublesome settlers to the government and hard neighbors to the Indians." In placing an estimate upon the opinions of Logan, respecting the Irish emigrants, regard must be had to his position at the time in the government. He had so long enjoyed a commanding influence in the affairs of this government, under Quaker rule, that he was jealous of any power that would thwart him in measures and policy, or impair his influence. There were parties under the provincial government, as well as under that of the Commonwealth. The Governor had his friends and partisans and the Assembly theirs; whilst the Council went with one or the other as they were inclined. Between these there were conflicts in the exercise of their respective powers that were marked with feeling and excitement. Logan was the leader of the Proprietory party and had to encounter often opposition and defeat from the Assembly. The Irish and Scotch vote in the Province was becoming larger, and commanding, and often exercised control in the election of members of Assembly and other officers. Logan had occasion to know its power and opposition, and would have preferred an unbroken influence in the Council and in the measures of government. He was generally in opposition to Governor Keith, decidedly the best and most popular of the Proprietory deputies, and was thus arrayed against the popular will, of which the intelligent and patriotic emigrants of Ireland and Scotland were influential exponents. There is much reason to believe that it was this limitation on his power in the government, that made him hostile to Irish and Scotch emigration, and led him to speak disparagingly of their character, as well as disposed to adopt the policy of restraining their emigration into the Province, by prohibition or taxation.

His declaration was "that the common fear is, that if they continue to come, they will make themselves Proprietors of the Province." He would have preferred that the government should continue permanently under the rule of the Quaker party, though the population of the Province could be numbered by hundreds, and its cultivated lands by a hand-breadth.

A like prejudice was exhibited about the same period, in another quarter, against the German influence in the Province. The influx of German emigrants was so great as to cause alarm to some politicians. It was feared by them "that the numbers from Germany, at the rate they were coming, in 1725–'27, will soon," as Jonathan Dickinson expressed himself at the time, "produce a German colony here, and perhaps such an one as Britain once received from Saxony." Jonathan Dickinson was respected for integrity and intelligence, having the public confidence. He had held the offices of Chief Justice of the Province, Speaker of the Assembly, and member of Council. This apprehension led to the imposition of a tax, by the Assembly, on German emigrants, to discourage their emigration to this Province.

Even the great, liberal and sagacious Franklin, allowed prejudice to influence his gigantic mind, in the view which he took of the German population of Pennsylvania, when, in 1755, he addressed the British public in favor of excluding any more Germans from the colonies.* Franklin, we might suppose, would have discriminated between the intelligent, moral and industrious portion of the German population, that were desirable as settlers, for good and useful habits, and who in time would comprehend their relations to a new government and conform to its requisitions, and the immense swarms of Palatine Boors who were landed in the Province, ignorant, indolent, unruly and vicious.

In those days of party divisions and dissensions, this eminent and patriotic statesman did not escape reproach and calumny in high places. "Governor Morris, under the influence of angry feelings, accused Franklin to the ministry, of using his office of Post Master General, to obstruct the King's service; and to the Proprietories, of the design of wresting from them the government."† Franklin devoted his time and labor to the discoveries of science and to promote the prosperity and welfare of his country, and lived to establish a reputation for genius, ability, integrity and patriotism that is imperishable. Time and experience reconciled him, and the wise and good of all parties, to the great acquisition in the German emigration, for the growth, resources and prosperity of Pennsylvania as a Province and State.

A representation unfavorable to the character of the Mennonites was made to Governor Gordon in 1727: "That a large

* Spark's Franklin. Vol. 7, p. 71.

† Gord. 330.

number of Germans, peculiar in their dress, religion and notions of political government, had settled on Pequea and were determined not to obey the lawful authority of government; that they had resolved to speak their own language, and to acknowledge no sovereign but the great Creator of the universe." Opposition was made to their admission as citizens, and it was not until 1741, that a law was passed for their naturalization. They had declared their readiness to pay their taxes and that they were subject to those in authority.

From their conscientious scruples against bearing arms, they did not enter the army to fight the battles of the country, but when Independence was acknowledged and a new government organized and established, they were obedient in all things to its requisitions. They have ever been in Pennsylvania a peaceable, industrious and moral community, paying their taxes regularly, avoiding strife, and living in peace with all men, with whom they had intercourse. They never allow the poor members of their society to be a public charge, but support them in the society.

The Quakers, who had a majority in the Assembly, and who could and did control its Legislature, in the early history of the provincial government, were subjected to severe strictures, for their neglect and unwillingness to provide for the defence of the frontier of the Province, against the many cruel murders perpetrated by the Indians on the inhabitants.

The numerous petitions of the inhabitants of the frontier in 1754, after the defeat of the Virginia troops under Washington, and again after Braddock's defeat in 1755, imploring from the provincial government measures for their defence and protection, had but little regard from the majority of the provincial Assembly, and led to the adoption of no efficient measures for the relief of the alarmed inhabitants and their families; and when the Indian war broke out in all its fury, along the extended frontier of the Province, and carried massacre into hundreds of defenceless families, sparing neither age nor sex, the government had not furnished a single soldier, arms or ammunition, either for the defence or aid of the frontier.

The inhabitants of the frontier finding that their repeated

applications, as well as their unmitigated sufferings from exposure to savage enemies, were disregarded by the majority of the Assembly, though Governor Morris had pressed upon their attention, the measures of defence, demanded by every obligation of duty, as well as humanity, in 1756, their memorial was sent to the King, and Royal government, respecting the defenceless state of the Province, and praying the interposition of the King, for the protection which was withheld from them by the Assembly of the provincial government. The petitioners, as well as Assembly complained of, were heard by their agents and respective counsel, before a committee of the Privy Council of the Royal government. That committee, after consideration, by their report which was approved by the Board, "condemned the conduct of the Assembly in relation to the public defence since the year 1742." Their expressed opinion was, that the Legislature of Pennsylvania, as of every other country, was bound by the original compact of government to support such government and its subjects. That the measures intended for that purpose by the Assembly, were improper, inadequate and ineffectual, and that there was no cause to hope for other measures, whilst the majority of the Assembly consisted of persons, whose avowed principles were against military services, who, though not a *sixth* part of the inhabitants of the province, were, contrary to the principles, the policy and the practice of the mother country, admitted to hold offices of trust and profit, and to sit in the Assemblies without their allegiance being secured by the sanction of an oath. This report was adopted by the Privy Council and a copy directed to be sent to the Province.*

The repeated complaints of the inhabitants, against the remissness and neglect of a Quaker Legislature to provide for the defence of the frontier, were thus sustained by the Royal government. When the opinion of the ministry on the conduct of the Quakers was communicated to the Provincial Assembly, some of the members of that society resigned their seats. Others declined re-election, and some flattered they could reconcile their consciences with the measures of the Assembly.

---

* Gordon's Hist. 337, 339.

The dissensions between the inhabitants of the frontier interior of the Province, who were mostly of Scot or Irish origin, with the Quaker party, were still continued with excited feelings and prejudices, on both sides. The Scotch Irish freemen complained whilst they had increased greatly in numbers, and were opening out the wilderness, and extending cultivation, as well as defending the frontier of the Province at the expense of their blood and lives against the Indians and the French allies, who were the public enemy of the country, they were without the assistance and protection from the provincial government, to which they were justly entitled, and amongst the grievances complained of, influencing the legislation of the Assembly to their prejudice, was the inequality in 1764, in the representation of the counties, the three counties of Philadelphia, Chester and Bucks, with a Quaker population having twenty six representatives, whilst the counties of Lancaster, York, Cumberland, Berks and Northampton had collectively but ten members.

The dissatisfaction existing between the Scotch and Irish inhabitants and the Quakers under the provincial government, was the occasion of criminations and recriminations. The Quakers charged the Scotch Irish with being haters of the Indian, inimical to him and as exciting the Indian wars by their encroachments; whilst the Scotch and Irish inhabitants, in their memorial to the Royal government, charged the Quakers with secretly supporting the Indians, by holding treaties and correspondence with them during the war; "and of having bestowed on them arms, ammunition and tomahawks, even when they were murdering the frontier inhabitants."* The opinions and accusations of both parties, were made, it is believed, under a cloud of prejudices, excited by partisans, with discolored representations, and founded on slight evidence, weighed in scales held by a partial hand.

Time and experience proved the policy advocated by politicians of distinction in the Province, of restraining the emigration of both the Irish and Germans, into the settlement of its wild land, to be so short sighted and contracted, that, if adopted,

Gordon's Hist. 422.

would have been ruinous to the fundamental interests of the Province and its government. The opinion of such politicians deserves but little regard, in their estimations of the principles and character of whole and numerous classes of their fellow-men, who are commended or censured as they accorded with, or opposed their views or purposes, in times of party excitement, when there is a contest between such leaders for official power and influence. Their opinions receive their bias and coloring from their own selfish feelings, and fluctuate with the rise and fall of parties.

Had the policy advocated by Logan, Dickinson and Franklin been adopted, as a permanent one, in the provincial government, of restraining emigration, by which the population demanded for its security and prosperity, and which has elevated it to the highest rank in the American colonies, was to be excluded the privilege of an asylum on its territory; these excluded emigrants would have sought permanent homes in other colonies, and the growth and improvement of Pennsylvania have been greatly retarded.

Without the aid, strength and resources afforded to Pennsylvania by its emigration of Irish, Scotch and Germans from 1725 to 1750, who would have been the pioneers of its immense wilderness, opened out its unbroken forests, cultivated its lands, and, in the infancy of the Province, reared so many habitations for Christian families, or erected in the "back woods" so many edifices, dedicated to the worship of the God of their fathers? Without such emigration, before the Indian wars, the frontiers of the Province would have extended little beyond the Schuylkill, and the citizens of Philadelphia, with their wives and children, would have been exposed to the torch, hatchet and scalping knife of the savage, and their midnight murderous assault and slaughter, and the Kittochtinny valley in its length and breadth, have remained a wilderness. Without such emigrants and their descendants, how few would have been found in Pennsylvania the advocates of American Independence and resistance to Royal usurpation and tyranny, and who would have filled up the ranks, or commanded the armies of Pennsylvania in the war of the Revolution, in which the liberties of the American people were defended and their independence established.

A more impartial age has expunged from historical record the prejudices and aspersions, which, in the early history of this Province, were cast on the German population, or the Society of Friends, and they have been allowed to pass almost into oblivion, and if recalled, it is only to make known the occasion of their existence and the temper, feelings and rivalry which brought them to life. Both of these great classes of the early settlers of the Province, are respected and commended for their virtues and usefulness.

Why is it, that a like liberality and justice, are not extended to the Scotch and Irish settlers of Pennsylvania and their descendants ? Why is time not allowed to cast a shade over accusations against them, which had a like origin in party rivalry, and no better foundation, than bad temper and perverted judgment ?

Were their evil deeds so many, and great that the mantle of charity can neither conceal nor cover them ? If so, where is the evidence of them ?

They were men, who laid broad and deep the foundations of a great Province, and who, with a master's hand, erected a structure of Government that was stable, capacious and elevated; whose prosperity and greatness commands admiration, and which, by public accord, constitutes the great Key Stone of the political Arch of the American Union.

The men, who were instrumental in this structure of government, with its free institutions, of religious and civil liberty, were more than ordinary men, to hold the plough and handle the axe, or ply the shuttle. They had other qualities, we would infer from their works, than enterprize, energy, bravery and patriotism, and they were not surpassed, for lofty virtue and consistent piety.

When we survey the Kittochtinny valley, between the Susquehanna and Potomac, with its cultivated and improved farms, flourishing towns and villages, its church edifices, in which Christian worship, and ordinances, are regularly observed —seminaries of learning of every grade, its high intellectual, social and moral condition, and remember that little more than one century since, the same valley was a wilderness—its population the Indian hunter, and its habitations the hut of the savage or the dwelling of the beaver, are we not led to inquire, who, under God, were the authors of this great work? A large portion of the population of this valley, at the present time, are the descendants of its first settlers. Do they not feel, that to their ancestors and their memory, they owe a debt of endless gratitude, for their works and services? Are they not interested in knowing and proclaiming the principles, that guided the first settlers in making this valley the abode of civilization and the homes of an intelligent, enterprizing, religious and moral community? Who is it, that now shares the common blessings, that result to the now comfortable and independent occupants of this delightful free valley, from the privations, toils, sacrifices, persevering industry, and virtue of the men, who dwelt in it when a wilderness, and transformed it to cultivated fields, meadows and gardens, with commodious and elegant dwellings, that does not feel an interest in knowing the character of those who accomplished so much, for those of this generation and their posterity? Other communities of the same Scot and Irish origin, have, at an early period, peopled other parts of Pennsylvania, whose progress, improvement, principles and virtues, were attended with the same happy success and prosperity, as characterized this portion of the Kittochtinny valley. The Scotch and Irish element was here more universal, and extensive, and embracing a larger community of the same religious creed, and forms of worship, and of the same homogeneous tastes and principles.

The character of the people who first settle any country, or establish their government, generally determines that of their descendants. Such is our estimation of the character, principles and habits of the first Irish and Scotch settlers of this Province, that all their descendants may, we think, be satisfied to have their character measured by the same standard. What Pennsylvania is, as a great and prosperous State of free Institutions, she owes to the mass of her original settlers.

Justice has not been done to the Scotch and Irish race, in

the Histories of the American Colonies and States. In some instances they are slighted, and in others traduced. For permitting this without rebuke and vindication, their descendants are not free from censure. The character of their ancestors is part of their inheritance, which they are bound by every obligation of duty, to reverence and defend.

To the Puritan settlers of New England there has been a different measure of justice, respect and honor. Their principles, virtues, institutions and public usefulness, have not only been recorded on the pages of History, but in numerous eulogies and addresses, on the return of the anniversary of the Landing of the Pilgrims on Plymouth Rock. Whilst the sons of New England, unite yearly, in bearing their testimony and tribute to the purity and transcendent merits of their ancestors, the descendants of other races, throughout the Republic, concur in honoring their memory, and in commemorating their principles and virtues. There were errors and public wrongs that were reproachful, imputable to some of the first settlers of New England ; chargeable to individual communities and arising out of the state of the country, prejudices, excitement and delusions ; but Historic truth does not require, that they should be permanently recorded to their reproach, without an exhibit of the extenuating circumstances, under which they originated, and, much less, that the misdeeds of individuals, or of a limited community, should be proclaimed as a stigma on the whole Puritan race, of the New England colonies. Blemishes that might be found, in the early history of these colonies, have been allowed to pass into oblivion; and lost in the effulgence of the mass of excellence, which adorned the character of many, of the early settlers of New England.

To the credit of New England men, they have led off in paying an early tribute, to the memory of their ancestors, by recording and perpetuating their principles, patriotism and public usefulness. Such was the position of the colonies of Massachusetts, and Connecticut, during the Revolutionary contest, and the War of Independence, that their history and that of their inhabitants, in earlier times, are matters of national interest, and deserving of national gratitude, and reverence. Whilst we accord to the early settlers of New England, great merits, and eminent usefulness, it is believed that the Scotch and Irish early settlers of Pennsylvania, Virginia and North Carolina, in energy, enterprise, intelligence, patriotism, religious and moral character, the maintenance of civil and religious liberty and in inflexible resistance of all usurpation in Church or State, were not surpassed by any class of settlers in the American colonies. Has this high character been regarded, and acknowledged as it deserved, by the compilers of History in Pennsylvania? It has not. Some compilers of local history in Pennsylvania, have accorded to the Scotch and Irish early settlers, religious and moral character of a high standard, as well as great public service and usefulness; whilst the authors of some historical collections and memoirs have indulged in wholesale accusations to their reproach.

The aspersions cast upon the ancestors of the mass of the best citizens of this State, require investigation, and that the accusers furnish the evidence to which they refer, in order to sustain their calumnies. From the acquaintance of the writer with the character of the Irish and Scotch settlers, who were the early actors in the settlement of the Province of Pennsylvania, he affirms that the accusations and reproaches thus imputed to the Scotch Irish race in Pennsylvania, are unfounded and unjust.

If such accusations, to the reproach of our ancestors, who have been in their graves for a half century or more, be allowed to pass without contradiction or refutation, time and repetition may give them currency and credit: and the fair fame of the men who had high claims on the country and posterity, for a life of labor, industry, toil, sacrifices and peril, in its improvement, defence and prosperity, may be unjustly prejudiced in the estimation of readers, who may take their opinions from an author, who has adopted some stale and selfish prejudice, which, in its origin, had neither foundation, credit, nor influence.

Mr. Sherman Day, in his Historical Collections of Pennsylvania, (in 1843, page 23,) in speaking of the Scotch Irish, says, they were "a pertinacious and pugnacious race," "pushing their settlements upon unpurchased lands about the

Juniata, producing fresh exasperation among the Indians. Massacres ensued, the settlers were driven below the mountains and the whole Province was alive with the alarms and excitements of war."

The only approach to a specification, is by Mr. Day, wherein he charges upon the Scotch Irish, the encroachments upon the unpurchased lands of the Indians about the Juniata, and the massacres and war, which ensued from these encroachments. For a charge so grave and reproachful, as being the authors of the savage war, that desolated the border settlements of the Province, the reader is not referred, by Mr. Day, to either dates, events, or any historical record, or document to verify the accusation. We are unwilling to believe, that Mr. Day had any dispositión to misrepresent the Scotch Irish of Pennsylvania ; but as his historical work was a hasty compilation of much general and local history, opinions and statements may have been adopted, without full investigation, and the prejudices and misrepresentations of the leaders or classes, opposed to the Scotch Irish race in the Province of Pennsylvania, received as veritable history, in which he was misled, and his publication made the instrument of wrong and injustice, to a numerous and most respectable class of citizens.

The wars between the Indians of Pennsylvania and its white inhabitants, did not occur before 1755, the year of Braddock's expedition and defeat. Then, and for some years preceding, the Scotch and Irish emigrants constituted the great mass of the effective population of the Province. They were settled in great numbers in various parts of the county of Lancaster, on the south eastern and western borders of York county, in the county of Northampton, and formed nearly the entire population of the Kittochtinny valley, in the county of Cumberland, between the Susquehanna, and the Potomac rivers. As the cession by the Indians, in 1736, of their claim to lands west of the Susquehanna and to the Kittochtinny mountains, as a western boundary, together with the adjustment, in 1737, of the temporary line between the Provinces of Pennsylvania and Maryland, left this great valley, between these rivers, open to settlement; the influx into it of substantial settlers of Irish and Scotch origin, was great, after 1737, and continued, with little abatement, for many years. Yet, with all this influx of settlers and appropriation of land, it is believed, that in 1750, more than one half of the arable land, in this valley, desirable for both fertility and other advantages, was still open to entry and settlement. At that time, there were in the Kittochtinny valley, about one thousand families, and in the counties of Cumberland and Franklin, which embrace this part of the same valley, it appears by the United States Census of 1850, that there were then in occupation 4,089 farms. From the condition of this valley, as an agricultural district, it is manifest, that, in 1750 and before, there was vacant land within its boundaries, that was suitable and desirable for a settler, greatly beyond what was required, to satisfy the wants or reasonable demands of emigration. It does not appear from Provincial records, that the Indians, at any time, complained of the settlements in the Kittochtinny valley, west of the Susquehanna. These settlements were made under licenses from the Proprietory government, before the cession, with the approbation of the Indians, and after the cession, by official grants in the regular form from the Land Office, to which Indian consent was not wanting.

The complaints by the Indians of encroachments, by the white inhabitants, on their unpurchased lands, were in 1742, and after; and were confined to illegal settlements on lands in Tulpehocken, on the Juniata, Aughwick, Path Valley and on Licking Creek, near the Potomac river, which embraced the Big and Little Coves. These settlements, with the exception of Tulpehocken, were in a mountainous country, extending from the Susquehanna to the Potomac, a distance of eighty miles, being west of the Kittochtinny mountains, and most of them west of the Tuscarora. Mr. Day, in the extract from his History recited, referred only to the Juniata, as the locality of the Scotch Irish encroachments, which were so offensive to the Indians. There is the highest authority, being that of R. Peters, Esq., Secretary of the Provincial Government, in his Report to the Governor, that the first settlers, who entered on the unpurchased lands at the Juniata, were Germans,* and

* Vol. 5. Col. Rec. 445.

were followed by some Irish emigrants, and at the visit of Mr. Peters, he found but six. The settlers who entered on the lands at Tulpehocken, before the purchase, were German Palatines, who came from the Province of New York.†

The settlements in Path valley, Sherman's valley, and Aughwick, were made up of a few families of Irish and German origin ; whilst those on the Licking creek hills, near the Potomac, were by settlers, most of whom came from Maryland and claimed under Maryland rights, and consisted of emigrants from Ireland, Scotland, Wales and Germany.‡ The provincial boundary line, having been extended by survey only to the summit of the Kittochtinny mountain, it was still uncertain how much of the Licking creek hills or coves were within the boundary and jurisdiction of Pennsylvania, which was not established until by the Mason and Dixon Line in 1767. It was on this district of uncertain jurisdiction that the Indians, with their French allies, made their first bloody and murderous slaughter of the defenceless settlers and their families, in October, 1755.

Immediately after the organization of the county of Cumberland, in 1750, the Provincial government took measures for the removal of the settlers west of the Kittochtinny and Tuscarora mountains. Richard Peters, Esq., Secretary, with the aid of the magistrates and sheriff of Cumberland county, repaired to the several places of settlement, being accompanied with delegates from some of the Indian tribes, and an interpreter. The measures of these officers were effective. The settlers were required, to abandon their dwellings, which were destroyed and burned, and compelled to enter into recognizances for their appearance at the next Court in Cumberland county, to answer for their breach of the Law. The settlers disclaimed right, acknowledged their offence and acquiesced in the requisitions of the magistrates, and the destruction of their houses, with the exception of one man, who resisted with threats, and was disarmed and imprisoned. The number of settlers found at these several places, amounted

† Vol. 3, Col. Rec. 323. In all visited by R. Peters and Magistrates, 62.
‡ Vol. 5 Col. Rec. 445.

to sixty-two. To whatever class of emigrants they belonged, they could not be considered as either "pertinacious," or "pugnacious." Their possessions were in the wilderness, remote from the settlements, and if lawless and disposed to resist the officers of the law, and oppose their purposes, it might easily have been effected. They were submissive, and under the most trying circumstances of a summary expulsion, with their families, from their dwellings, which were burned in their presence, they were left in an unbroken mountain forest, without a habitation or shelter of any kind, for their families. The secretary and magistrates executed this public duty, with fidelity to the Indians and Provincial government, and with as much lenity to the settlers, as the execution of the law would allow.

The magistrates of Cumberland county who assisted in the performance of this painful duty, were of Scotch or Irish oriigin or descent; and were under no legal obligations to leave their homes in the Kittochtinny valley and seek offenders against the law, by traversing the wilderness for more than fifty miles, and crossing rugged and elevated mountain ranges, by the Indian or Trader's path, and then impose, and execute summary, rigid punishment on men and their families, for a transgression of the laws, arising out of the indulgence of the proprietory government, and their ignorance of the law and its penalties.

Benjamin Chambers and George Croghan, two of their Justices, and who were of Irish nativity, without the aid of Mr. Peters, visited the settlers, eleven in number, on Sherman's creek, and adopted and executed the same measures for their removal, and the destruction of their houses. Whatever sympathy they may have felt for them, some of whom, no doubt, were their countrymen, yet their sense of public duty, made them enforce the law, whilst they had to witness the great distress of poor sufferers in its execution.

Such is the history from public documents of the encroachments by the white settlers on the unpurchased lands in Pennsylvania, west of the Kittochtinny mountain, and the measures for their removal. When examined by an impartial and intelligent enquirer, can they discover anything to warrant the imputation, to the whole Scotch Irish race, in the then Province of Pennsylvania, the wrongs committed by a few misguided settlers, who, with most peril to themselves and their families, from both the Indians and government, ventured to settle in the wilderness on unpurchased lands. The great mass of the Scotch and Irish settlers, who were cultivating and improving their farms, in the remote parts of the Province, knew no more probably of the existence, or acts of these settlers, than they did of their countrymen who might be taking up an abode in other colonies or continents.

Even the inhabitants of the Kittochtinny valley, which was the settlement of civilization nearest them, were in no respect responsible for their acts or character. They were separated from them by ranges of lofty mountains, and in place of encouraging their Scotch, or Irish friends, or acquaintances, to make settlements, where they would be exposed to Indian hostility, as well as contravene the law, would have directed them to their own attractive valley, where there was abundance of fertile vacant land, and where it was desirable as well as politic, to increase the numbers and strength of the settlement, by every accession of peaceful and industrious freemen. We affirm it to be illiberal, and unjust, to reproach the Scotch Irish settlers of Pennsylvania, as a race, with being regardless of the forms of the Land office and laws, pushing their settlements upon unpurchased lands, to the exasperation of the Indians, because some few individuals of that race, with emigrants from other countries, may, under an infatuation that is unaccountable, and with an adventurous spirit that was reckless, have ventured upon some of those lands remote from the settlements.

The insinuation, that these encroachments were the exciting cause of the war, waged by the Indians on the white inhabitants of the frontier settlements, is not supported by public documents. The Indians in 1742, and for some years after, did complain of these encroachments. The measures of the government in 1750, in removing the settlers, and the destruction of their dwellings by public authority, in the presence of some of the Indian tribes, were significant evidence of the energy and sin cerity of the government, to restrain such encroachments, and punish the trespassers; and though these efficient measures did not entirely prevent further encroachments by a few roving adventurers, it had a tendency to discourage and restrain it, as well as to reconcile the Indians, who were but little incommoded or interfered with, by the few settlers who placed themselves, on the unpurchased lands, when it was their interest and safety to avoid strife with the Indians.

Whatever dissatisfaction they might still have, and exhibit, was quieted, and removed by the Treaty, and cession at Albany, in 1754. The lands, on which encroachments, had been made, west of the Kittochtinny, were an acknowledged part of that cession, which the Indians understood, and intended to be embraced by it, and for which alone they said they had received remuneration.

The most early, frequent and continued subject of complaint by the Indians, in their conferences with the Proprietory, his agents or the officers of the Provincial government, was the "long tolerated usage of Traders, *licensed* by the government, carrying to their towns and trading posts, *rum and other intoxicating liquors*, for traffic, by sale or barter—many of the Indians, under the influence of this drink, were tempted to part with all they had for it, to their degradation and ruin," were excited to broils, bloodshed and murder, and when restored to sobriety, they found themselves deprived of their skins and furs, and were left without anything of value, to clothe themselves or their families, or to procure the ammunition necessary to enable them to resume the chase. Their destitution made them desperate, and ready to embark in any project, though of peril, when there was any hope of plunder or reward.

The Governor of Pennsylvania, in his message of 1744, says: "I cannot but be apprehensive that the Indian trade, as it is now carried on, will involve us in some fatal general war with the Indians. Our traders, in defiance of the law, carry spirituous liquors amongst them and take the advantage of their inordinate appetite for it, to cheat them of their skins and their wampum, which is their money, and often to debauch their wives into the bargain. Is it to be wondered at then, if, when they recover from their drunken fit, they should take some severe revenge?"*

Though the provincial laws forbade the traffic in intoxicating liquors with the Indians, under severe penalties: and proclamations were issued almost annually, by the Governor against it, calling on the officers of the government to enforce the laws, yet so great were its profits to the trader, and so tempting to the poor infatuated sons of the forest, that this vile trade remained unabated, and was pursued by the white traders under license from the Governor to trade, regardless of the law and its penalties, and of the evils inflicted on the Indians.

The injuries done to the Indians, by a few white settlers, putting up their cabins and clearing and cultivating a field, or a corner of the wild lands of the Province, on which the Indians claimed the right to hunt, were but light and trivial, compared to those inflicted on their nations, by the traffic in intoxicating liquors, tolerated by the government and practised by unprincipled white men.

The great dissatisfaction of the Indians in Pennsylvania, was with the Government of the Province, and the Proprietory agents, arising out of the cessions of land obtained from them within the Province. The boundaries of some of these cessions were obscure and uncertain, and yet so comprehensive, as to embrace half the Province. It is not to be supposed, that there was any design in this, on the part of the Proprietory or his agents, that advantage might accrue to the Proprietory from the obscurity.

As there was a great inequality in the capacity of the contracting parties, in both intelligence and power, it behooved the Proprietory and his officers, to use abundant caution in making the terms of the cession clearly intelligible, to the ignorant and feeble savage. The lands should have been bounded by a description, referring to natural boundaries, that could not be mistaken, or be open to future cavil.

The cession of 1737, by the Indians, conveying lands on the Delaware, was "to *extend back into the woods, as far as a*

Vols. of Penn. Arch. Vol. 3, p. 555.

man can go in one day and a half." What a hook was here left to hang a controversy on. The Indians soon after, expressed their dissatisfaction with a boundary so uncertain, and when the walk was made, it only tended to increase the dissatisfaction. The white walkers selected, were so expert and indefatigable, that the Indians who were to accompany them, complained that they could not keep up with the white men who ran.* The wound made by the agents of the Proprietory in Indian confidence by this treaty, and the claim and execution of it, remained long an open one, and could scarcely be said to be healed, when the more comprehensive and important treaty and cession were made at Albany in 1754, between the Proprietory of Pennsylvania and officers, and the six nations, which swept from under the feet of the Indians, nearly all the lands claimed by them within the Province, in consideration of the small sum of £400 pounds. The Indians could not have understood this wholesale disposition of this claim to their hunting grounds. When they came to consider where they stood, and how little was left to them of their wide domain, their dissatisfaction was intense and general, but more particularly with the Delawares, a small, but formidable tribe. They alleged, that they only intended to cede the lands unsold on which the *settlers had encroached*, which did not form a tithe of what was embraced in the Albany cession.

To the Indians, the encroachments of the few white settlers on the hills, and in some of the small valleys west of the Kittochtinny mountains, were but a small grievance. The white settlements on the east side of those mountains, would make the hunting grounds on the immediate border of little value, as the game would seek more retired woods, and the Indians had for many years before these settlements withdrawn from them. The acts of the settlers were individual wrongs, not

---

* The Proprietory agents had advertised in the public papers for the most expert walkers, to make the walk, offering a *reward* of five hundred acres of land in the purchase, and £5 in money, to the person who should attend and walk the farthest in the given time. The walkers desired, entered on this novel race on time, through the woods, and though supplied with refreshments at points, without rest or loss of time, one of the white men sank down exhausted, under the effort, and one only was able to continue until the exhaustion of the time.—*Day. Col.* 508.

justified under any pretended right, and which the Proprietory government was bound to redress, and which its agents declared should be redressed, by government authority. But the wrongs done the Indians, by the officers and agents of the Proprietory and Provincial government, were on a much more extensive scale. They were by public authority, in whose acts the Indians had reposed confidence, and they were not to be satisfied, that the marks of a few Indian chiefs to a single instrument of writing, which they could not read, was to be an absolute, legitimate and conclusive transfer of their nation's claim to the lands of half the Province, and for any wrong or fraud perpetrated on them by the public agents, they were without appeal to or redress by higher authority.

The dissatisfactions of the Indians, under the compact of 1754, were continued without redress from the Proprietory, or the Provincial government; and they were allowed to grieve over their lost hunting grounds and the homes of their families, taken from them by the public agents and officers of a government, they had regarded as their friend and protector.

The French, who were aspiring to dominion in North America, at the expense of the English possessions, were extending rapidly their posts and fortresses, from the northern lakes into the valley of the Ohio. Every art and device was used by them, to attach the Indians to their influence, and withdraw them from English alliance. They, by the line of their fortifications, were more in the neighborhood of the Indian towns and hunting grounds, which were to them places of trade and barter, for supplies adapted to their condition and wants. The Indians had an opportunity of seeing their armaments, and military stores, as well as to witness their enterprise, promptitude and perseverence to further the purposes of their government. They did not admire the pacific temper of the Provincial government, and the few English forces which they had seen before 1755, in the Provinces of the English government, did not impress them much in favor of the power of the government, or of the bravery and intrepidity of its soldiers.

The French ingratiated themselves by presents, and marked attentions, that were captivating ; whilst they endeavored to impress on them the suspicion that the English, whose settlements were extending from the Atlantic westward, were intended to be permanent, and take from them all their hunting grounds, whilst they drove them to the extremity of the land.

The extended dissatisfaction with the English, that followed the Albany cession, was opportune for French influence, which was at once artfully used, to withdraw the Indian nations from English to French alliance. The vast territory obtained and claimed by the Proprietories of Pennsylvania, under the Deed of 1754, was to the Indians a confirmation of the suspicions, that the French had endeavored to excite, as to the design of the English to take their lands. The French, at a crisis when they were preparing for hostilities, were successful in bringing to their alliance, the Indians within the Province of Pennsylvania, with the exception of a small number. The French posts and garrisons now became places not only for Indian resort, but of organization and armament, for the approaching war. Indian hostilities were soon witnessed, with a vengeance and unparallelled success in the defeat of Braddock. In a few months after, they waged a cruel and merciless war on the defenceless settlers and their families of Pennsylvania; also simultaneously on those of Maryland and Virginia. The cause of that hostility could not be mistaken. For a twelve month it had been rankling in the breast of every Indian warrior. Their dissatisfaction was notorious, and yet the Proprietory of Pennsylvania and the Provincial government slumbered amidst the indications of an approaching war, without any efficient measures to avert it or to provide for the defence of the frontier.

The constituted authorities of the Province understood well, at the time, the cause of the Indian hostilities, with which the inhabitants were visited. They did not attribute them to the encroachments of the few Irish, Scotch or German settlers on the unpurchased lands, many of whom, with their families, had fallen victims to the savage warfare to which, from their location, they were exposed. The responsibility for these hostilities was to be charged to those in power and authority in the Province.

Gov. Morris, in his address to the Assembly, of Nov., 3, 1755, expressly tells them, "that it seemed clear, from the different accounts he had received, that the French had gained to their interest the Delaware and Shawnese Indians, under the ensnaring pretence of *restoring them to their country.*"

At a treaty at Easton, in 1756, the Governor desired to know of the Indians the cause of their hostile conduct. Tudyuscung, chief of the Delawares, and who represented several nations, replied, "I have not far to go for an instance; this very ground, that is under me," striking it with his foot, "was my land and inheritance, and is taken from me by fraud. When I say this ground, I mean all the land between Toheccon creek and Wyoming, on the river Susquehanna."

The Assembly, in their reply to Gov. Denny, in June, 1757, say, "It is rendered beyond contradiction plain, that the cause of the present Indian incursions in this Province, and the dreadful calamities many of the inhabitants have suffered, have arisen, *in a great measure,* from the exorbitant and unreasonable purchases made, or supposed to be made of the Indians, and the manner of making them—so exorbitant, that the natives complain that they have not a country left to subsist in."* This fact was known to the Royal government, which interposed its influence with the Proprietories of Pennsylvania, and desired that the Indians should be conciliated on the subject of the boundary of the Albany cession. This was done at Easton, in 1758, by a Deed from the Proprietories by their agents, abridging the bounds of the conveyance of 1754, and which released to the Indians the lands situate northward and westward of the Allegheny mountain.

The Proprietories of Pennsylvania, in their dealings and negotiations with both natives and settlers, were just, honorable and generous. They were incapable of any fraud, or imposition, and did not allow it to be practised by their agents. Their disposition to accommodate the settlers, made them indulgent to them for the small amount of purchase money asked for their lands, and made them tolerate many irregularities in the acquisition, and evidence of appropriation of land from

* 2 Smith's Laws, 120.

regard to the wants and necessities of the settlers and exigency of the time. A fair settlement, prosecuted with ordinary diligence, without regard to the efficient forms of grant of land provided for and required, was yet tolerated and recognized as valid as if obtained and prosecuted, in all the form required for official grants.

In their negotiations with the Indians, the Commissioners appointed by the Proprietories, were instructed "to conduct themselves with candor, justice and humanity." They ever manifested their wishes to conciliate them by probity and kindness. As the residence of the Proprietories, was most of the time in England, the management of the affairs in the Province, was necessarily committed to their agents, on whose representations they were, in a great measure, dependent for information respecting the measures in the Province. They would no doubt sometimes be misled by the representations of their agents, and redress for alleged wrongs to either the Indian nations or the white settlers, would, in consequence of the absence of the Proprietories from the Province, and the few and tardy channels of communication there were between the Province and England, be delayed, to the injury and dissatisfaction of all parties. There would have been no war between the Indians of Pennsylvania and its inhabitants, had it not been for the war waged between the English and French governments, a part of which was transferred to the American continent, where both governments were ambitious of extending their dominion. Into this conflict the Indians were brought by the French, who had been most successful in 1755 in seducing them into their alliance. The prominent and influential cause placed before the Pennsylvania Indians, to excite them against the English, and the Provincial government of Pennsylvania, were the wrongs inflicted on them under the Albany cession. The exciting cause of Indian hostilities immediately before, and after Braddock's defeat, is to be traced not to the encroachments of the few white settlers, but to the more extensive wrongs by the government and its agents.

The settlers and their families on the frontier, being nearest and most defenceless, were the first victims to the attack, in which the Indians were encouraged by Braddock's defeat, Dunbar's flight with the remains of the army, and the omission of the Royal and Provincial governments to provide measures for the defence of the Province, against the terrible incursions of the savages, which were to be apprehended; and were soon realized in the murder, and slaughter of the inhabitants, of numerous settlements, without regard to age, sex or condition.

CHAPTER II.

Detraction of Scotch Irish by Mr. Sargent—Vindication required—Where did they reside?—Who and what were they?—Religious and moral character—Religious organization—Institutions of learning—William Tennent, Senior—Blairs—Finley—Davies—Allisons—Smiths, and others—Settlement in York Barrens—The men from that settlement—in Donegal—Paxton—and in western part of York county, now Adams.

In the introductory memoir to the Journal of Braddock's expedition, by Mr. Winthrop Sargent, published within the last year in Philadelphia, by Messrs. Lippincott, Grambo, & Co., the author has taken occasion to refer to the Scotch Irish race in Pennsylvania, in terms so opprobrious, as to call for notice. He says: "They were a hardy, brave, hot-headed race; excitable in temper, unrestrainable in passion, invincible in prejudice. Their hand opened as impetuously to a friend, as it clinched against an enemy. They loathed the Pope as sincerely as they venerated Calvin or Knox, and they did not particularly respect the Quakers. If often rude and lawless, it was partly the fault of their position. They hated the Indian, while they despised him; and it does not seem, in their dealings with this race, as though there were any sentiments of honor or magnanimity in their bosoms, that could hold way against the furious tide of passionate, blind resentment. Impatient of restraint, rebellious against any thing that, in their eyes, bore the semblance of injustice, we find these men readiest among the ready, on the battle fields of the revolution.

If they had faults, a lack of patriotism or of courage was not among the number."*

This concentrated denunciation, of a numerous race, has a meagre qualification in the preceding page, when it is stated, that, in each of the classes referred to by the author, "were to be found men of education, intelligence and virtue."

For this measure of reproach and opprobrium cast upon the ancestors of a large portion of the inhabitants of Pennsylvania and other States, there is no reference to authority or facts. The author does not accord to them integrity, enterprise, religious or moral character. The character thus imputed to men, who did much for the improvement and prosperity of the Province and State of Pennsylvania, and for the defence of civil and religious liberty, as well as for the free institutions and independence of the Republic, is at variance with all that is generally received, as matter of historical truth. It is true, that error and mistatement on a subject of such interest, should be corrected, if they exist. Accusations and reproaches, if unfounded, are to be refuted, and the character of men who deserved well of society and their country, should be vindicated.

Character is said to be transmissible, and that the character of descendants, may be determined by what was that of their ancestors. If this be so, it is of interest to inquire into what, in truth, was the character of the Scotch, and Irish, early settlers of the Province of Pennsylvania, that their descendants may know themselves, as well as the character of their ancestors. The descendants of the early settlers in Pennsylvania, of Scotch, or Irish origin, have nothing to apprehend from the investigation, to the prejudice of their ancestors or themselves. To this wholesale denunciation of the Scotch Irish race in Pennsylvania, by Mr. Sargent, we propose to reply, by inquiring, where these settlers were in Pennsylvania, and who they were, and what they were?

The accusations made against the men, who were actors in this Province at "the time that tried men's souls," are to be

* His. of Brad. Exp. 77.

met by the history of the settlements, made, in the infancy of the Province, by the emigrants from Ireland and Scotland, with their energy, progress, intelligence, religious and moral character, social condition, religious, educational and patriotic tendencies.

Their ancestors were not without faults; they were men with their infirmities, and made mistakes. Individuals of the race have done wrongs against society, and their brethren, but not to a greater degree, than were perpetrated elsewhere, in civilized communities of the same number in like circumstances. The offences of a few infatuated, vicious or turbulent men, under a feeble government, are not to be imputed as a lasting stigma and reproach to all, of the same foreign origin, dwelling under the same government.

As well might the respectable families of emigrants, who are in these days coming to our land, as their future abode, be identified with the fugitives from justice, and liberated felons, who may have got a passage in the same steamer. Into the Province of Pennsylvania, for many years, were shipped from Ireland and Germany, great numbers of ignorant and poor subjects, who were unable to pay their passage, and were sold into service for a term of years to the colonists, for the amount of their passage money, and were called "Redemptioners." They were held in service by the farmers and others, to assist in the labor required in the towns and country, some of whom became useful and respectable citizens, but many were low and vulgar, and of disorderly and vicious habits. The English government, by its authority, for a time, transported to the colonies many of its convicts, against the wishes, interests and remonstrances of the colonists, as well as against the public peace and welfare.* In the most orderly communities, into which a portion

* By British policy, the American colonies were made an asylum for the worst of felons, transported to them. Those persons, who, by their enormous crimes, were unfit for society in England, were to be let loose on society in America, and be deemed fit servants for the colonists, and that their labor and industry, might be the means of improving the said colonies, *more usefully to his majesty*. Both Virginia and Maryland passed laws in restraint of this transportation, which were disallowed by the King and Council, as derogatory to the Crown and Parliament. The colonies had still to endure the evils of this vicious system from the mother country, for a considerable time, without

of such material should be infused, it might be expected; that there would be occasional exhibitions of vice, violence, and crime, to the annoyance of the public, under a new government, with few officers, in an extended and wild territory.

The first emigrants, from Ireland, to the Province of Pennsylvania, came, about the beginning of the last century, and settled in and near Philadelphia, in the counties of Bucks, Chester, and several parts of Lancaster. They were Protestant Christians, of the Presbyterian denomination, and as characterised them and their Scotch associates, wherever they formed a settlement, as soon as they had reared, or obtained houses for their families, they organized congregations for Christian worship. For this purpose, they habitually assembled themselves together, holding to the government, creed and doctrines, of their fathers, as contained in the Westminster Confession of Faith, with its Catechisms, as the rule of Faith and ecclesiastical organization, which they intended to maintain for themselves and their children; and which they reverenced, as the offspring of the religious liberty, that they sought to found, in a Province settled under a Charter, that proclaimed religious freedom and equal rights.

They had fled from civil oppression and religious tyranny, in the land of their fathers, and they hastened, in their new homes, to manifest their sincerity and regard for their privileges, under a government of free institutions, and limited powers, by erecting their houses of public worship, called "meeting houses," dedicated to the only true God. Not being satisfied long with a licensed ministry, that afforded them occasional supplies, they sought, and had settled Pastors, of learning and piety, installed to the office of their Christian minister, who was to go in and out before the people, and administer the received ordinances of the Church.

The first Presbyterian ministers in this country, were nearly all men of liberal education. Some had received their ed-

remedy. It is said, about 1750, not less than from three to four hundred felons were annually brought into the State of Maryland.† These convicts had, after they landed, the run and choice of the colonies before them.

† British Empire in Am. Vol. 3, page 23.

ucation in the Universities of Scotland; some in Ireland, and a few at one of the New England Colleges. Though there was a great demand for ministers, in the rapid settlement of some parts of the Province, by emigrants of the Presbyterian denomination, yet, from Dr. Alexander's research, there would seem to have been but one instance, of introducing into the ministry, of that Church, a candidate, without a college or university education, and that was under extraordinary circumstances.

The first Presbyterian church organized, with a place of public worship, was in Philadelphia, in 1703, and in the next year, or year after, a Presbytery was formed, called the Presbytery of Philadelphia. In 1716, the Presbyterian body had so far increased, that a Synod was constituted, consisting of four Presbyteries, viz: Philadelphia, New Castle, Snow Hill, and Long Island.

"After the formation of the Synod, the body went on increasing, receiving additions, not only by emigrants from Scotland and Ireland, but also from natives of England and Wales, who came to the middle colonies, and were thrown by circumstances, into the neighborhood of Presbyterian churches, and also from natives, or their descendants, of France, Holland, and Switzerland, who preferred the Presbyterian form of worship or government. To these, may be added, a number from New England, who were induced, by local considerations, or other circumstances, to connect themselves with the Presbyterian body."*

As the Irish and Scotch emigrants, generally, preferred agriculture, to other occupations, they located themselves in the rural districts, on lands open to appropriation in the Province, or by purchase from some earlier settler. In consequence of this rural taste, and settlement, Presbyterian influence and increase were more manifest, and extended in the country, than in the city.

Settlements of Scotch Irish were made on the banks of the Octorora creek, Lancaster county, in 1717. "They and their

---

* Dr. Miller on Presb. Ch., Ency. Rel. Knowl.

descendants," says Mr. Rupp, in the History of Lancaster county, by him compiled and published, "have always been justly regarded as amongst the most intelligent people of Lancaster county. Their progress will be found to be but little behind the boasted efforts of the colony at Plymouth."* They had for their pastor the Rev Andrew Boyd, who preached to them in 1724. This testimony to the character of the settlers on Octorora, is not from one who can be suspected of partiality, from any affinity to the Scotch Irish, but from an impartial historian, of German descent, and German religious associations.

A number of emigrants from Ireland, settled about 1720, or before, in Bucks county, north of Philadelphia. They shortly after their settlement, organized Presbyterian congregations. One of them became of notoriety in the Province, in having for its pastor, the Rev. William Tennent, Senior, who received a call to the Presbyterian congregation on Neshaminy creek, in 1726, which he accepted. He was an emigrant from Ireland, and had been in connection with the established Church, but shortly after his arrival in America, he renounced his connection with it, and joined the Presbytery of Philadelphia. He was celebrated for his profound and accurate acquaintance with the Latin and Greek classics. At the time he was engaged with his pastoral charge at Neshaminy, there existed no college or academy, of a high order, in the middle colonies, where young men, seeking the ministry, could obtain the necessary learning. About the beginning of the last century, a public school was established at Philadelphia, by the Society of Friends. Its first preceptor, George Keith, though a man of genius and learning, yet, being eccentric and restless, he left the school, after a year, and, so far as we can discover, it did not flourish, or acquire any celebrity. To obtain a qualification, young men, desirous of entering the Presbyterian ministry, were obliged to go to Scotland, or New England, for their education, and there were few candidates in the Presbyterian connection, who were able to bear the expense of an education, at places so remote.† William

* Rupp's His. Lan. 439. † Whitfield's Journal.

Tennent, resolved to supply this destitution, as far as he was capable, by opening a school for the education of young men, in the knowledge of the classics, as well as in divinity. For this, no man was better qualified, by attainments, as well as his ability and aptness, as an instructor. His school was established, and in operation, in 1726. The building for it, was erected by him, a few steps from his dwelling, and was made of logs, from the forest near it. It, and its principal, were visited by the celebrated Rev. George Whitfield, who traversed this country. In speaking of the building, he says, "the place wherein the young men study now, is called, in contempt, 'The College;' it is a log house about twenty feet long, and near as many broad, and to me, it seemed to resemble the school of the old prophets, for their habitations were mean. All that we can say, of most of our universities, is, they are glorious without. From this despised place, seven or eight worthy ministers of Jesus, have lately been sent forth, more are almost ready to be sent, and the foundation is now laying for the instruction of many others."*

The Hon. Elias Boudinot, LL. D., who knew Mr. Tennent well, says: "That he was well skilled in the Latin language, that he could speak and converse in it, with as much facility, as in his vernacular tongue, and also, that he was a proficient in the other languages." His general character appears to have been that of a man of integrity, simplicity, industry and piety. Such was the reputation of the man, who assumed to establish the first place and means of education in the colony, above that of the common school, in which only the rudiments of education were taught. Whilst he discharged his pastoral labors to his congregation faithfully, "in season and out of season," at the same time, his learning and talents were devoted to the education of the young men, who sought their intellectual improvement, and religious training, under his teachings.

At such a time there was no project, so desirable for the best interests of the Province, as to raise the standard of edu-

* Whitfield's Journal.

cation within it ; and Mr. Tennent was the very man for the work. With the aid of his eminent son, Gilbert, for a time, who was also a native of Ireland; and who received his education under his father, the school was opened, and conducted with success, and great usefulness. The health of William Tennent, Senior, declined in 1743, and he died in 1746, aged 73.

The character of this school, and its founder, is further attested by the attainments, and reputation of its pupils. Plain and unpretending, as was the edifice, "a log cabin" in the woods, with the minister of the neighborhood for Principal and Teacher, and with opponents who ridiculed the experiment, by giving to the school, in derision, the name of "the Log College," yet, it attracted young men of studious habits, who applied themselves with diligence. It was also blessed by Providence, in having for its pupils, young men of superior talents, who left it with minds cultivated, disciplined and stored with knowledge, that qualified them for the study of any of the learned professions. The young men of this school, prosecuted their studies as preparatory to the ministry, on which they entered. "Amongst these pupils, educated in that school, were the four sons of the Principal, all of whom were members of the Presbyterian Church. Gilbert Tennent was ordained as a pastor in 1727. He is supposed to have been the first candidate licensed in the Presbyterian Church, who was educated within its limits."* Mr. Whitfield, in his journal of his visit to the American colonies, says: "I went to the meeting house to hear Mr. Gilbert Tennent preach ; and never before heard I such a searching sermon. He went to the bottom indeed, and did not daub with untempered mortar. He convinced me more, that we can preach the Gospel of Christ no further than we have experienced the power of it in our hearts. Hypocrites must either soon be converted or enraged at his preaching. He is a "son of thunder," and does not regard the face of man. He is deeply sensible of the deadness and formality of the Christian Church, in these parts, and has

---

* Alexander's Log College, 43.

given noble testimonies against it." It has been remarked, by an eminent divine, "that higher testimony and from higher authority could not be given upon earth, and that it is doubtful, whether Mr. Whitfield had ever expressed so high an opinion of any other preacher of any denomination."

In 1744, Mr. Gilbert Tennent established a new Presbyterian Church in Philadelphia, chiefly composed of those, who were denominated the converts and followers of Mr. Whitfield. Dr. S. Miller says, "he was a bold, ardent, practical and unusually impressive preacher. He died in 1764, in the 62nd year of his age."*

One of the most distinguished men educated at the Log College, was the Rev. Samuel Blair, a native of Ireland, who was among the first pupils of this institution. After finishing his classical and theological studies, he put himself under the care of the New Castle Presbytery, by which he was licensed to preach the Gospel. Soon after he was settled in the Presbyterian congregation at Shrewsbury, New Jersey, where he labored for five or six years. From this, in 1739, he received an earnest call from a Presbyterian congregation of Scotch Irish settlers, in New Londonderry, otherwise called Fagg's Manor, in Chester county, Pennsylvania. When he received this call, he left it to the Presbytery to decide, whether he should go or stay. He was advised to accept, and went, and was installed as the pastor of this congregation, in 1740. Shortly after, he established at this place a classical school, of the character of that before instituted at Neshaminy, by Mr. William Tennent, Sr., where he received his education. His school had particular reference to the study of Theology, as a science. He was esteemed as one of the most able, learned, pious, excellent and venerable men of his day; was a most profound divine, and a most solemn and impressive preacher. To his pupils, he was himself an excellent model of pulpit eloquence. In his life, he gave them an admirable example of Christian meekness, of ministerial diligence, of candor and catholicism, without a dereliction of principle. He was emi-

* Miller's Life of Rogers.

nently serviceable in the part of the country where he lived, not only as a minister of the Gospel, but as a teacher of human knowledge. From his academy, the school of the prophets, as it was frequently called, there came forth many distinguished pupils, who did honor to their instructor, both as scholars and Christian ministers."* Under his ministry at New Londonderry, there occurred a remarkable revival of religion. "As a preacher, there was a solemnity in his very appearance, which struck his hearers with awe, before he opened his mouth. He spoke as in the view of eternity, as in the immediate presence of God." The opinion entertained by the eloquent and pious Mr. Davies of Mr. Blair, as a preacher, was given to Mr. Davies' friends, who, on his return from Europe, were curious to know his opinion of the celebrated ministers, whom he had heard in England and Scotland. After dealing out liberal commendations on such as he had most admired, he concluded by saying, "that he had heard no one, who, in his judgment, was superior to his former teacher, the Rev. Samuel Blair."† Very great assemblies, would ordinarily meet to hear Mr. Blair on any day of the week, and often times a surprising power accompanied his preaching, which was visible, among the multitude of hearers. Mr. Blair, in a communication to a friend, in speaking of his congregation, says: "Except in some singular instances of behavior, which, alas! proceed from, and show, the sad remains of original corruption, even in the regenerate children of God, while in this imperfect state, their walk is habitually tender and conscientious, their carriage towards their neighbors just and kind; and they appear to have an agreeable, peculiar love one for another, and for all in whom appears the image of God."‡

Among the students at Mr. Blair's academy, was the Rev. Samuel Davies, born in the county of New Castle, State of Delaware, in 1721. He received the greater part of his academic and theological education under the teaching of the Rev. Samuel Blair, and was licensed to preach in 1745. He was eminent for eloquence, piety and learning, and acquired

* Miller's Retr. 2, 343. Ency. Rel. Knowl.

† Miller's Life of Dr. Rodgers. ‡ Log College. 183.

a reputation so well known for genius, and taste, that it is not deemed necessary to dwell on them here. Having settled as Pastor of a Presbyterian congregation in Virginia, shortly after he was licensed, where he remained for some years, admired, respected and useful, in 1759 he was elected President of Princeton College, in which situation, he remained but eighteen months, being removed by death in 1761, in the thirty-seventh year of his age.

The Rev. John Rodgers, who was born in Boston, of Irish parents, at the age of sixteen, entered the academy, under the care of the Rev. Samuel Blair, where he pursued his classical and theological education, and finished his theological studies, under the direction of the Rev. Gilbert Tennent, in Philadelphia. In 1747, he was licensed by the Presbytery of New Castle, and gave in his public ministrations, as well as in his exemplary private deportment, indications of the future excellence and usefulness for which he was happily distinguished.

As associates of Davies and Rogers, at Blair's academy, were Mr. Alexander Cumming, one of the ministers of the Presbyterian Church in New York, and who held a high place among the ministers of the day; also Messrs. Robert Smith, James Finley, Hugh Henry, and a number of others, who became distinguished in the ministry.* The health of the Rev. Samuel Blair, gave way, under the labors of his ministry, and school, and death removed him from both, in 1751, at the age of thirty-nine.

The Rev. John Blair, the brother of Samuel, was also an alumnus of the Log College; where he received his education, and as a theologian, was not inferior to any man, in the Presbyterian Church, in his day.

He was ordained in the pastoral charge of three congregations, in the Kittochtinny valley, west of the Susquehanna, as early as 1742, before Cumberland county was erected, and when the district was a part of Lancaster county. His pastoral charge embraced the "Big Spring" congregation, (now Newville,) and some other congregations in the new settlement.

* Miller's Life of Rodgers.

But as the incursions of the Indians, after Braddock's defeat, dispersed the inhabitants, Mr. Blair retreated to the eastern part of the colony. He accepted a call from Fagg's Manor in 1757, which had been formed under the ministry of his favored brother Samuel. Mr. Blair discharged the duties of his ministry, and conducted a flourishing Grammar school at this place for about nine years, where he prepared many young men, for the ministry. He was afterwards chosen Vice President of Princeton College, and Professor of Divinity, which places he filled with great ability, fidelity and reputation. He died in 1771, in the fifty-second year of his age.

One of the most eminent men in the Province of Pennsylvania, in its early history, was Dr. Samuel Finley, President of Princeton College. He was born in Ireland, where he received part of his classical education, and arrived in the Province in 1734. It is believed that he finished his education at the Log College, as there was then no other institution, in the Presbyterian Church, where young men were prepared for the ministry; and he was under the care of the New Brunswick Presbytery, most of whose members were educated in that school. He was licensed in 1740. After he was ordained as an evangelist, for some years, he visited various parts of the country, where the inhabitants were most destitute of religious instruction; and it was said, much success attended these itinerant labors of this pious and talented minister. That Dr. Finley was an accomplished scholar and skilful teacher, was universally admitted. In 1744 he accepted a call from Nottingham, in Chester county, adjacent to Maryland, having a congregation of settlers resident in both Provinces. In this place he instituted an academy, with the view chiefly of preparing young men for the ministry. This school was conducted with admirable wisdom and success, and acquired a higher reputation than any other in the middle colonies, so that students from a great distance were attracted to it. Some of the most distinguished men in our country, laid the foundation of their education, eminence, and usefulness in this academy; amongst whom were Governor Martin, of North Carolina, Dr. Benjamin Rush of Philadelphia, his brother, Judge Rush,

Ebenezer Hazard, Esq., Rev. James Waddel, D. D., the eloquent and blind preacher of great celebrity in Virginia, Dr. McWhorter of New Jersey, Col. John Bayard and Governor Henry of Maryland. There were no better classical scholars formed anywhere in this country, than in this school. The method of instruction in the Latin and Greek languages, was thorough and complete. The temper of Dr. Finley was remarkably benignant and sweet, and his manners affable and polite. The degree of doctor of divinity was bestowed on him by the University of Glasgow, which seems to have been the first instance of any Presbyterian minister in America, receiving that honorary distinction.

In 1761, he was elected President of Princeton College, and entered on the duties of that station, in which he was distinguished for wisdom and efficiency. He died in 1766, in the fifty-first year of his age.* "Dr. Finley was a man of sound and vigorous mind, of extensive learning, and of unusually fervent piety. Seldom has a life been more exemplary, or more useful."†

In the early history of Pennsylvania, there was no man of more eminence and usefulness and worthy of historical notice, than Francis Allison, D. D. He was born in Ireland, and after an early classical education, at an academy, completed his studies at the University of Glasgow. In 1735 he came to America, and was appointed pastor of a Presbyterian congregation at New London, Chester county, Pennsylvania. About 1741 his solicitude for the interests of the Redeemer's kingdom, and his desire of engaging and preparing young men for the ministry, and of promoting public usefulness and learning, induced him to open, at New London, a public school. There was, at the time, a great want of learning in the middle colonies, and he generally instructed all that came to him, *without fee or reward.* The Synod of Philadelphia assumed the patronage and supervision of this school, and allowed Mr. Allison a salary of £20 a year, and his usher £15, and called on their congregations to contribute, for a time, to the support of

---

* Dr. Alexander's Log College, 204. † Dr. Miller's Life of Rodgers, 57.

the school. In 1747, Mr. Allison, by solicitation, took charge of the Academy in Philadelphia, and in 1755 was elected Vice Provost and Professor of Moral Philosophy in the College, which had just been established. He was then also minister of the first Presbyterian Church. Besides an unusually accurate and profound acquaintance with the Latin and Greek classics, he was well informed in moral philosophy, history and general literature. To his zeal for the diffusion of knowledge, Pennsylvania owes much of that taste for solid learning, and classical literature, for which many of her principal characters have been distinguished. The private virtues of Dr. Allison conciliated the esteem of all who knew him; and his public usefulness, has erected a lasting monument to his praise. In his public services he was plain, practical and argumentative, warm, animated, and pathetic. He was frank and generous in his natural temper; warm and zealous in his friendships, catholic in his sentiments, and the friend of civil and religious liberty, abhorring the intolerant spirit of persecution, bigotry and superstition, together with all the arts of dishonesty and deceit. His humanity and compassion led him to spare no pains or trouble, in relieving and assisting the poor, and distressed, by his advice and influence, or by his own private liberality. His friend and successor, Rev. Dr. Ewing, said of him, that he was "one of the brightest luminaries that ever shone on this western world;" and the venerable Dr. Alexander has given his opinion "that Dr. Allison was one of the most accomplished scholars who had adorned the Presbyterian Church in the United States." He continued in the discharge of his laborious duties until his death in 1777 ; aged 72.*

There was an extensive settlement made by Scotch Irish emigrants about 1720, on the Pequea and its tributaries, in the county of Lancaster. The Rev. Adam Boyd was commissioned to collect a congregation at that place, which he did, probably about the time he was settled as a pastor over upper Octorora, which was in 1724. The congregation at Pequea was, for years, under the pastoral care of Rev. A. Craighead, and

* Enc. Ret., Miller's Rel., Alexander's Log Col.

his successor, the Rev. D. Alexander, until 1750, when the Rev. Robert Smith, D. D., was installed. He labored faithfully, not only as the pastor of this congregation, but gave a portion of his time and labor to the congregation at "the Run," after, and now known as the "Cedar Grove Presbyterian church." Dr. Smith was not only a faithful pastor, but one of talents, learning, and piety. Having received his education at the Log College, like many others educated there, he directed his talents, and attainments, to the instruction of others. He established at Pequea a classical and theological institution of a high character, about a half mile from the church. At this school, amongst many others of usefulness, were educated the three sons of Dr. Robert Smith. Here was laid the foundation of the eminence of his son, Rev. Samuel S. Smith, D. D., President of Hampden Sidney College in Virginia, and afterwards President of Princeton College, where he presided for eighteen years, with great ability, being eminent as a scholar, author, and for pulpit eloquence. At Pequea was also born Dr. Smith's second son, Rev. John Blair Smith, who received there his education, and succeeded his brother, as President of Hampden Sidney, and was afterwards the first President of Union College in Schenectady. He was an eloquent, evangelical and successful minister. At the same place, was born and educated, the Rev. William Smith, the third son, who was a pious and judicious minister, and though less distinguished, than either of his other brothers, yet, in the opinion of his good father, "to comfort and edify the plain Christian, he was equal to either of them."* Dr. Robert Smith, after a life of labor and great usefulness at Pequea, for forty-two years, died, at the age of seventy. The labors of such a pastor, and instructor, for such a period, must have been blessed to the conversion, and edification of many of the community, where he labored.

The Rev. Patrick Allison, D. D., was born in Lancaster county in 1740, and received his education in the College of Philadelphia, and was installed pastor of the Presbyterian

* Log College by Alexander, 200.

church in Baltimore in 1762, where he remained honored and useful until his death in 1802, in the sixty-second year of his age. Dr. Allison held a place in the very first rank of American clergy. He shone with distinguished lustre in the judicatories of the Church. For the perspicuity, correctness, sound reasoning and masculine eloquence of his speeches in ecclesiastical assemblies, he was long admired and had scarcely an equal."*

To the extended list of eminent men of Irish origin or descent, already presented, distinguished for usefulness in the Province of Pennsylvania, in its early history, might be added that of the Rev. Charles Beaty, a native of Ireland, who had received there a good classical education, and which he extended and finished at the Log College, and being licensed to preach by the Presbytery of New Brunswick, was settled as Pastor of the church at Neshaminy, left vacant by the death of the venerable founder of the Log College. Rev. Mr. Beaty was engaged much in missionary labors about 1745, visiting destitute Presbyterian settlements. Dr. Alexander says, he was an able, evangelical preacher, and was much esteemed for his private virtues and public labors. He was distinguished for public spirit and popular address. He died on the Island of Barbadoes, where he was taken sick in collecting funds for the aid of the College at Princeton in 1772. The Rev. John Ewing, pastor of the first Presbyterian church in Philadalphia in 1759, graduated in the College of New Jersey, and was elected Provost of the University of Pennsylvania in 1779, and died in 1802, in the seventy-first year of his age. Dr. Miller said that "the eminent character of this gentleman, the vigor of his talents, the extent of his learning, his extraordinary accomplishments, at the head of a literary institution, and his excellence as a preacher, is well known."

To appreciate the value of the labors and usefulness of the learned public benefactors, referred to, it is necessary to have in view the times and circumstances, under which they appeared, and in which they were actors. The Province of Penn-

* Miller's Life of Rodgers, 179.

sylvania was in its infancy; with a government, simple, experimental and inefficient for the maintenance of its laws; with an extensive territory, nine-tenths of which, was a wilderness; whose population was made up of emigrants from different countries; with finances inadequate to the purposes of government, and with its Proprietary, who was the owner of the soil, possessing great control in the government, yet, during the greater part of the time, residing in England. At such time, this Province was blessed, in having within its borders the eminent men, of whose lives a sketch has been given; classical and scientific education were not provided for in any institution by government, or by any associations contributing funds to its support.* It was left to individual enterprise to supply the destitution, and at this crisis, William Tennent, Sr., was the individual, under Providence, first to apply his talents and acquirements, to the experiment of establishing a school under his care, for the classical, scientific and religious education of young men. Though his undertaking was ridiculed, as presumptuous and visionary, yet, as narrated, it was eminently successful. That success is fully attested by the brief history of the men educated in that school, who, for learning, eloquence, piety and usefulness were not surpassed, in their day, by the educated men of this or any other country. The influence of the Log College Institution, and of the kindred ones established and maintained by some of its pupils, in elevating and extending education, sanctified by the teachings of the Bible, with its precepts of the Law and Gospel, was incalculable for the best interests of the Province. A warm and earnest Christianity, was the animating spirit of these humble seminaries, which was infused into most of their pupils, and made them the instruments of religious and moral instruction to others.

---

* At the beginning of the eighteenth century, Colleges in the colonies did receive but little patronage from England, and were dependent on the labors, enterprise, literary and benevolent efforts of a few individuals. In England many said, "Let the colonists attend to the production of the earth, and look to England for learning and learned men." When pressed on the subject of religion in the colony, one of the lords of trade implicated a curse upon their souls, and said, "let them make tobacco."—Foote's Virg., 151.

During the first half of the last century, where were there in office or station, under government, men whose services or usefulness to the community, were to be compared with that of the founders of the schools referred to? There were politicians and office holders, who were more conspicuous, whose power and patronage commanded influence and attention, yet much of their time was passed in the routine of prescribed, subordinate, official duties, or in intrigue to maintain and advance their power and interests. The best and most prominent of the men in the Provincial government, were then, in a great measure, engrossed with frivolous controversies between different departments of the government, about the legitimate exercise of their respective powers, and to the neglect and prejudice of the public interests. The men who signalized themselves at this period, by their acts of public usefulness, were the founders and conductors of the institutions for education described. They were men of learning, piety, and great purity of character, who appreciated education, and deplored the want of suitable institutions for it, as required by a rapidly increasing and destitute community. They were poor Presbyterian ministers of Scotch Irish nativity or descent. Having neither silver nor gold to give, in founding institutions for the intellectual, moral, and religious improvement of the people, they gave what they had, their time, labor, talents, and learning. They planted and watered, and, under God, their work prospered; the fruits of which were gathered and enjoyed, not only in their own day, but by generations, then unborn.

Extensive settlements, by respectable emigrants from Ireland and Scotland, were made in other parts of Lancaster county, than those already enumerated. They had their ministers of the Gospel and their schools, but not of the eminence of those described. The settlement in the district, which we presume, received its name of Donegal, from the origin and choice of the settlers, was extensive, embracing a large district of fertile and choice lands. As early as 1726, this settlement had progressed so far in improvement and organization, as to have ths Rev. James Anderson, from Ireland, as their pastor, the church being called that of "New Donegal." In

1732, the increase in the number of Presbyterian congregations, induced the formation of another Presbytery in Pennsylvania, which was called the Donegal Presbytery. Its jurisdiction embraced the frontier settlements, and though its boundaries became, in the progress and increase of population and the Church, reduced, it still exists under its ancient name. From the township of Donegal, many respectable settlers sought to improve their circumstances, by removing into the Kittochtinny valley, west of the Susquehanna, and some made their homes in the southern colonies, in the same extended valley, which made Donegal a place of note, in the distant south.

In the history of York county, by Messrs. Carter & Glossbrenner, it is stated: "That about the years 1734–35 and 36, families from Ireland and Scotland settled in the southern part of the county of York, (then Lancaster county) and what is known as the "York Barrens." They consisted of the better order of peasantry; were a sober, industrious, moral and intelligent people, and were, for the most part, rigid Presbyterians. Their manners partook of that simplicity, kindness and hospitality characteristic of the class to which they belonged in their native countries. The descendants of these people still retain the lands which their respectable progenitors selected. And we are happy to add, that the present inhabitants, with the lands, inherited the sobriety, industry, intelligence, morality and hospitable kindness of their predecessors." This is the testimony of impartial compilers of history, to the character of the early Irish and Scotch settlers, who, with their descendants, have occupied for more than a century, a large portion of the county of York. Soon after the original settlement, they erected a church near Muddy creek, which, with the neighboring settlements of Presbyterians, was supplied by an approved ministry of the Gospel and its ordinances. To these settlements in the "Barrens," the seminary and classical school of Dr. Finley, at Nottingham, was so convenient of access, that young men, desirous of classical and scientific education, would be able to attain it there without inconvenience. That attention was given to education in these settlements, is attested by the eminence of some of its sons. It was from this Scotch Irish district of sterile soil, came the Hon. James Smith, a native of Ireland, who, as a youth in the family of his father, settled there. He received his education under the immediate care of the celebrated Dr. Allison, at Philadelphia. Mr. Smith was one of the most distinguished Lawyers of Pennsylvania, enjoying an extensive and lucrative practice, in York and other counties. He was a prominent member of the Revolutionary Congress, and one of the signers of the Declaration of Independence, as well as an active and efficient member of many important committees appointed by Congress. He commanded, as Colonel, a Regiment in the Revolutionary army, and was a practising lawyer for about sixty years. He died in 1806, at the age of 93, in the borough of York. From the same district, emanated Judge Hugh H. Breckenridge, well known for his classical attainments, his legal learning, and his ability, as a Judge of the Supreme Court of the State. Also, about the same time, the Hon. James Ross, of Pittsburg, distinguished and eminent, as a lawyer and statesman, and who, at the Bar, as a lawyer and advocate, or as a statesman in the United States, had no superior. Also, the Hon. John Rowan, who represented the State of Kentucky, in the United States Senate.

These men were of the Scotch Irish race, reared and educated in the Province of Pennsylvania, adorning the profession of the Law, in which they were engaged, and an honor to their progenitors, as well as to the State.

Pennsylvania furnished in its early history, from Scotch Irish families, men educated in the schools of Dr. Finley, Dr. Allison, and others, distinguished, not only in the ministry, but as lawyers, jurists and statesmen, and for their literary and scientific attainments. Thomas McKean was born in Chester county in 1734, his father being a native of Ireland. He acquired an accurate knowledge of the languages; of the practical branches of mathematics, rhetoric, logic and moral philosophy, under the tuition and direction of Dr. Francis Allison, preparatory to the study of the Law. His subsequent celebrity and reputation are so well known to the American people, as to require no detail. A summary here is sufficient. He was an eminent lawyer, and a member of the Revolutionary Congress, from its opening, in 1774, until the peace of 1783; a signer of the Declaration of Independence, President of Congress for a time, Chief Justice of the State of Pennsylvania, and Governor of the State for the Constitutional period.

Hugh Williamson, of Scotch descent, was born in Chester county, in 1735, and received his education at the College of Philadelphia, under the direction of Dr. Allison, where he graduated in 1757. He was a man of great scientific acquirements, eminent for talents as well as learning. He removed from Pennsylvania, before the Revolution, to North Carolina, which State he represented in Congress for several terms with ability, and was a Delegate to the Convention that framed the Federal Constitution, of which he was a decided advocate. His history of North Carolina, in three volumes, attests his erudition, ability and research.

David Ramsay, the American Historian, was born in Lancaster county, in 1749, the son of James Ramsay, a respectable farmer, who had emigrated from Ireland, and who, by the cultivation of his farm, provided for the subsistence and education of his family. His son, David, received his early education, in a common school, and in one of the academies of the country, and finished in Princeton College, where he graduated in 1765. Dr. Ramsay studied medicine at Philadelphia, where he graduated with great distinction; and was distinguished for abilities and literary attainments. Dr. Rush, who was intimate with him, said: "His talents and knowledge are universal. His manners polished and agreeable, and his behavior to all men always without offence; joined to all these, he is sound in his principles, strict, nay, more, severe in his morals, and attached, not by education only, but by principle, to the dissenting interest." The predominant trait in his character, was philanthrophy and piety, which influenced all his actions. He was the zealous advocate of American Independence, and attended the army in the capacity of Surgeon. Having removed to South Carolina, he represented that State in the Revolutionary Congress, and, during the absence of

John Hancock, President, presided for a year, with ability, industry and impartiality. His historical works, and other productions, form part of the permanent literature of our country.

Robert Fulton, the successful applier of steam to navigation, was born in Little Britain, Lancaster county, 1765, of respectable Irish parents, who removed to Lancaster borough, where he received a good English education. His attainments and inventions, bespeak the high superiority of his talents.

There was also a Scotch Irish settlement, at an early day, at Paxton, in the neighborhood of where Harrisburg is, county of Dauphin. This district was one of some notoriety, as near the frontier, where a ferry was established and maintained by Mr. Harris, for crossing the Susquehanna—a great public accommodation—as well as being on the great road from Eastern Pennsylvania, through the Kittochtinny valley, to Virginia, and the more southern Provinces. Traders, as well as Indians, met there for traffic and conference. It acquired also an ignominious notoriety, for the massacre of the Conestoga Indians, perpetrated by a few of its violent men. This deed was a barbarous one, and indefensible. Yet, it has been greatly exaggerated, without reference to the circumstances, that existed, to extenuate it. We shall take occasion to notice it more fully, before we terminate this vindication.

About 1737, emigrants from the North of Ireland and Scotland, settled in the north western part of York county, on the waters of Tom's and Marsh creeks, (now Adams county.) They were the first settlers in that district, which was separated from the Kittochtinny valley on the west, by a range of mountains about ten miles in width. These settlers were a highly respectable community, moral, energetic, industrious, and intelligent; of frugal and plain habits, but kind, friendly and hospitable. In their religious organization, they were Presbyterian, and as early 1740, missionary supplies were provided for them by the Presbytery of Donegal. It would appear, that they had settled on some of the choice lands, on the water courses referred to. Actual settlers had been invited and encouraged, by agents of the Proprietary, to make permanent settlements on the lands in Pennsylvania, open to appropriation. Though this form of title was at first objected to by some of the Proprietary agents, unless followed by an official grant, yet it soon became prevalent, and was recognized, and established, as of validity with the Land Office grants, and only yielded to priority. Many of the settlers on Marsh creek, had made their settlements on lands, that had been surveyed, or set apart for a Proprietary manor. These manors were reserved, from sale or grant, in the ordinary forms. As the lands were wild, unimproved, and were the property of the Proprietary, remote from the settlements on a frontier, the settlers might readily suppose that, like all the other lands, not appropriated by settlers, they were open to settlement. This mistake of the settlers, was the occasion of unpleasant difficulty and controversy, between them and some of the Proprietary officers.

Mr. Peters, as Secretary of the Proprietory, with some assistants, in 1743, went into this settlement, to survey the manor lines, which would include the settlements and improvements of a number, who, for years, had been expending their money, time, and labor, in clearing and improving their supposed homesteads. The settlers, in considerable numbers, forbade the Proprietary agents to proceed with the survey, and on their persisting, broke the Surveyor's chain, and compelled the party to retire. The settlers were prosecuted, but submitted, and accepted leases for a time, and purchased the lands before the leases expired, to the satisfaction of the parties interested. This resistance of the Proprietary agents, was deemed by them, a great indignity, and public offence, and the settlers implicated, were reproached as "lawless," by the Proprietary officers, and the opponents of the Irish, in the Province.

As these settlers had been in the actual and peaceable possession of the lands, they occupied for years, which were enhanced much in value by their labors, they had the legal right, by the common law, to retain their possession, and defend that possession until they were ejected by a superior title, under the Judgment of a proper Court, and by due course of law.

The resistance of these settlers, was not of the officers of the law, or its authorities. The rights of the Proprietaries, in regard to their lands, were like those of any other individual, or vender, and were to be construed according to their contracts, express or implied. The Proprietary was not the government; their agents were not public magistrates, and were liable to mistakes, and could, and often did, commit wrongs, which were redressed by their superiors. The resistance, on this occasion, was not a "public offence," if it only restrained the Proprietary agents from disturbing the peaceable possession of the settlers, until it should be adjudged, by a competent Court, that they were to be removed. It was no other wrong than is committed every day, by men who are in possession of real estate, by what they suppose a sufficient title, and who refuse to surrender that possession, on the demand of a claimant, until there is an investigation of that title, by the tribunal of the law. These Marsh creek settlers, as soon as they understood their legal relation to the Proprietary, and before any trial, acquiesced, and became tenents and purchasers, to the satisfaction of the Proprietary claimants. They were not, from principle, or habit, inured to passive obedience, irrespective of legal rights and authority, but as soon as the law was made manifest, they were obedient to its requisitions. Though the opponents of the Irish race, in the Province of Pennsylvania, were disposed to make much of this "Marsh creek resistance," to the prejudice of the Scotch Irish early settlers, as evidence of their turbulent and lawless spirit, it was because they had little to complain of, in a class of citizens, who took care to understand their rights, civil, religious, and political, and to maintain them, as well as respect the rights of others.

The inhabitants of this part of the Province, increased in numbers and resources, and extended their improvements and the cultivation of their lands. Several large Presbyterian congregations were organized and maintained, within their bounds, and as was done by their kindred, in other places, the school-house building soon followed the erection of their own habitations, and the school-master was abroad in their midst; and the minister of the Gospel, was to them, a watchman and shepherd, as well as their instructor.

Upon these settlers, and their families, was devolved the perilous duty of defending the whole settlement from the Indian incursions and ravages, in the wars, which followed Braddock's defeat, in 1755. The massacre and dispersion of the inhabitants of the Kittochtinny valley, during those wars, made Marsh creek settlement a frontier, and as the Indians crossed the Kittochtinny valley and its mountains, they both massacred, as well as carried off captive many of its inhabitants.

The hardy settlers of this district, were, necessarily, called out, to defend their families and habitations, against the incursions of savage and cruel enemies, that spared neither age, or sex. These settlers organized themselves into military companies, and in concert with the inhabitants of the Kittochtinny valley, pursued the Indians, in their retreats, to their hiding places, in the western mountains; whilst some of them formed a part of that gallant, brave, intrepid, and successful expedition, under the command of Col. Armstrong, which attacked and captured the Indian fort and town of Kittaning, on the Allegheny river, in 1756.

The men who had resisted the Proprietary agents, that came to survey their lands, on a claim for the Proprietary, periled their lives, in a distant campaign, across the mountains, to attack the Indians, and their French allies, and defend the lands and province of the Proprietaries of Pennsylvania, against the invasions and devastation of the enemy, whilst the agents and favorites of the same Proprietary, with few ,exceptions, took care, to keep themselves at a safe distance from the enemy, and dangers. These resolute settlers held on to their lands, as a permanent abode for their families, and when the war of the Revolution broke out, all of them having the ability to bear arms, responded, with alacrity, to the calls of their country, in defence of American liberty and independence. More willing or brave hearts, and higher patriotic feeling, were not to be found in the colonies.

After the close of the Revolutionary War, some of the descendants of these Irish settlers, sought homes in western Pennsylvania, and after the lapse of some more years, others emigrated further west, where they became prominent, respectable, and influential citizens of western States.

Many of the descendants of this race, remained on the farms, or in the neighborhood, where their ancestors had resided. Some cultivate the same farms, and worship on the same hill, or near the same spring, where those ancestors, more than a century since, were accustomed to assemble, with their families, for worship, with their Presbyterian brethren, according to their approved forms, and in the maintenance of venerated creeds.

These descendants, who dwell in the neighborhood of those early settlements, form an intelligent, religious, and moral community, of law abiding and conservative habits ; many of whom, have enjoyed, and still possess, political and social distinction, and are respected for enterprise, intelligence, and public usefulness.

CHAPTER III.

The attractions of the Kittochtinny Valley to Settlers—Who they were—Improvement and Progress—Religious and moral character of population—Church organizations—Frontier—Peaceable intercourse with Indians, until after Braddock's defeat—Exposure to Indian massacre and devastation—Neglected by government—Harassed by Indian Wars—Dispersion of inhabitants—Murder of Conestoga Indians in Lancaster county—Indian Traders attacked—Murder of Indians by Frederick Stump in Sherman's valley—His rescue and escape—Return of inhabitants to the Kittochtinny valley in 1765—*Their progress, increase and occupation.*

THERE was no district of country, in the Province of Pennsylvania, that had more to recommend it, to the early settlers, for agricultural purposes, than the valley of the Susquehanna, opposite Harris' ferry. It was known by its Indian name of the Kittochtinny valley, from the extensive mountain range, as its western boundary, called the "Kittochtinny," signifying "Endless mountains," extending through several of the Atlantic provinces. The Indian name of Kittochtinny, was, by the white population, softened, by dropping some of its consonants, and in general acceptation by them, after some time, called Kittatinny, which it retained, until supplanted by Cumberland, the name of the county. It is to be regretted, that it had not been allowed to retain its appropriate Indian name of Kittochtinny. That part of the valley, west of the Susquehanna, embraced, what now constitutes the county of Cumberland, and almost all of the county of Franklin. For fertility of soil, abundance of copious springs, clear running streams, variety of forest timber, luxuriance of vegetation, and salubrity of climate; presenting, as a boundary, on two sides, mountain ranges, with a wide valley, made up of hills, planes, and dales, it was not surpassed, by any of the American colonies. Attractive as it was, its settlement was retarded, from being a frontier, remote from the eastern settlements, the Indian claim to which, was not purchased by the Proprietary of Pennsylvania, until October, 1736. A great part of it was in controversy with the Proprietary of Maryland, who claimed the same as belonging to that Province.

To assert and maintain the claim and jurisdiction of Pennsylvania, to this valley, west of the Susquehanna, some resolute and enterprising citizens were induced, by the Proprietary agents of Pennsylvania, to make settlements in this district, under Pennsylvania authority, which was done in a few instances, as early as 1730–31, and were continued until January, 1734, when a commission was issued to Samuel Blunston, from the Proprietary of Pennsylvania, authorizing him to grant licenses, in writing, to settle lands west of the Susquehanna. They were an inception of title to much of the most desirable lands in the valley, extending from the Susquehanna, to near the Potomac. With those settlements, under Pennsylvania authority, the Indians were satisfied, as they had been with those before, made west of Wright's ferry, near York. Their tendency was to restrain encroachments, under Maryland authority. The Proprietary of Pennsylvania, acknowledged the Indian claim, and for some time, had been negotiating with them, for a cession of it, delay of which, was occasioned by the retirement of some of the five nations, to the western rivers or lakes.

That cession being obtained in 1736, and the Maryland controversy, being at the same time, suspended, by agreement of the Proprietaries of the two Provinces, the Land Office of Pennsylvania was opened in January, 1737, for the sale and appropriation of lands *west* of the Susquehanna, on the usual terms. The application for warrants, and the influx of settlers, were now great into this valley.

The settlers, who occupied this part of the Kittochtinny valley, under the license system, were from Ireland and Scotland. They were men of energy, enterprize, industry, and intelligence, being substantial farmers, with capital and resources, for improving and extending their farms. Their origin, character, and the attractions of the country, induced the emigrants of the same nationalities, to flock to this district of country. Some of these, had been resident for a time, in the eastern part of the Province, and sought now to obtain a permanent home in the Kittochtinny valley.

Though the frontier of the Province, it increased rapidly, and in 1750 had about 1000 taxables, its population being five or six thousand. Nine-tenths of the population were natives of Ireland or Scotland. There were a few respectable families of German Mennonites, settled east of where the town of Greencastle is now located, on the waters flowing into the Conococheague ; and also on the head waters of the Antietam. There were also some Germans, of substance and good character, who had settled near the Grindstone Hill, south of where Chambersburg is situated, belonging to the German Reformed Church, and a settlement of emigrants from Wales, on the Maryland boundary, on a stream of water flowing into west Conococheague, which gave to this stream, and the adjacent country, the name of Welsh Run, by which it is still known. There were some German families settled, at an early day, in the eastern part of the valley, near the Susquehanna.

The taste, of the early settlers of this valley, was rural, and the occupation looked to for their families, was agricultural.

They selected lands, with a view to permanent residence, and as the means of maintaining their families. The first dwelling house erected in the Conococheague valley, was at the mouth of the Falling Spring, of hewed logs, and covered with a lapped shingle roof, secured by nails, in the usual manner. Many of the dwelling houses, of the first settlers, were built of choice logs, hewed and well put together, two stories high, and with several apartments above and below ; and as early as 1744, stone dwelling houses, of two stories, were erected, in different parts of the valley ; some of which, are still standing, and comfortable residences for a family. The stranger, who came to view the land, was not regarded as an intruder ; but if of fair character, was received with warm hearts, and taken into hospitable families, and information and aid given to him, that would enable them to select lands that were eligible, and open to appropriation. Good, and convenient neighbors, were more desirable than extended territory.

The settlers, in their settlement, were engaged in extending their improvements, by buildings, clearing and enclosing lands for cultivation. They were characterized by enterprize, and persevering industry, and were generally of steady habits, religious and moral character. The great mass of them in this valley, being of Irish or Scotch nativity, had as their standard of Church organization, government, and creed, the Westminster Confession of Faith, with the Catechisms received from the Westminster Assembly. That standard was one on which their ancestors, and themselves, had stood and maintained in a foreign land, of religious intolerance, and which, in a land of religious liberty, they were not disposed to depart from.

As the settlements progressed, they were desirous of being supplied with a Gospel ministry, and as early as 1734, the Presbytery of Donegal sent supplies or missionaries into this valley, which, in their minutes is called the country, "Over the River." As the settlement progressed, under the "Blunston Licenses," congregations were organized in the years 1734–5–6, and 7. Before 1740, there were not less than eight Presbyterian congregations, organized in the valley, which had church buildings erected, for public worship, and most of them supplied by pastors, of their choice. The Presbyterian ministers, of that day, were nearly all of Irish nativity, and education. They were good classical scholars, as well as sound and learned theologians. Among the early ministry of this valley, was the Rev. John Blair, educated at the Log College, of whose life a very brief memoir has been given. He was settled at the Great Spring, as early as 1741, having the charge of that and some neighboring congregations.

Simultaneous with the organization of congregations by these settlers, was the establishment of school houses, in every neighborhood. In these schools, were taught little more than the rudiments of education, of which a part was generally obtained at home, under parental instruction. Reading, Writing, Arithmetic, Trigonometry, and Practical Geometry, were the branches to which attention was given. The Bible was the standard daily reader, by all classes able to read; and the Shorter Catechism of the Westminster Assembly, was to be recited, and heard by all in the school, as a standard exercise, on every Saturday morning.

The government of this extended community, was, in a great measure, patriarchial. The father was the instructor, and ruler of his household. Subordination to parents, was the universal education and training, and obedience was the settled habit of the youth of the family. The great instrumentalities, in the instruction of youth, were home, the school, and the Church. Religion was the great principle, on which was founded the early government of this people; the regulator of their families, their social and domestic habits. That religion, was that of the Bible, the fear and love of God, as the beginning of wisdom, and the keeping of his commandments, as taught in the Scriptures, as the great duty of man. In a community, without public magistrates, and officers of the law in the neighborhood; influence and rule, would be with the eldest, and wisest of the people, and which, by common consent, would be extended over the morals and actions of individuals. Public safety, peace and happiness, required this exercise of control by public sentiment, and respect for it would be accorded.

In 1735, by the order and appointment of the Court, the valley was divided into two townships, by a line crossing the valley at the "Great Spring," now Newville; the eastern one called, "Pennsborough," and the western one, "Hopewell," and a Justice of the Peace and a Constable, appointed for each. In 1741, the township of Antrim was established, embracing the Conococheague settlement, and what now constitutes the county of Franklin, with a Justice of the Peace and Constable for it.

These conservators of the peace, would be so few, over this extended country, as to afford but little aid to the maintenance of peace, order, and the authority of the laws. The great conservator and arbiter of right, would be the well regulated religious and moral sentiment of the community. The settlers were farmers, pursuing the even tenor of their way, in improving and cultivating their farms, rearing and educating their children, and providing for their schools and churches. The people were obliged to be a law unto themselves. Having emigrated from a country, where the common law was the standard of right and wrong, in the relations of persons, it, and its principles, would be applied in aid of the moral law, to the actions of individuals. The provincial government had its place of business, with its offices and officers, at Philadelphia; the only officers of this government, seen by the settlers of this valley, for many years after its first settlement, was the Deputy Surveyor, to survey and return their lands. Whilst the local county government, until 1750, was at Lancaster, a distance, to many of the inhabitants, of one hundred miles, or more, the officers of this local government, with which the people of the valley had intercourse, before that period, were the assessors and collectors of the public taxes. The Courts, for the trial of criminals, was so distant from a great part of the valley, as to afford but little protection to the inhabitants.

Yet the settlement of this division of the Kittochtinny valley, was expanding; its improvements progressing, and the comfort and resources of the inhabitants, rapidly increasing. This Scotch Irish settlement, was the most extensive of any in the Province, having in it, in 1748, about 800 taxables, dwelling in peace, and in the offices of good neighborhood with one another. During this period of patriarchal government, we do not learn, from history, or any public document, that any outrage was perpetrated within its bounds, by any riotous, or unlawful assembly, or any high crimes committed against the laws.

Predominant, as was the Scotch Irish element, in this settlement, with its numerous Presbyterian congregations, in every part of it; yet it was not intolerant, or a persecutor of the small Mennonite and German Reformed societies, that were in its midst, or of any other denomination, that was inclined to make their abode in the valley. They lived in harmony with all, as Christian brethren, interchanging the offices of good and obliging neighbors. The population of this valley, had, for their southern boundary, the Province of Maryland, with which the vexed question of the actual location of that boundary, before 1739, was unsettled. In 1735–6, the conflict between the inhabitants of the two Provinces, in the eastern part of the county of Lancaster, was harassing, attended with riot, breaches of the peace, blood-shed, and alleged murder, and where the settlers belonged to different classes of emigrants; yet, in the Kittochtinny valley, with settlers living near, and adjacent to, the place where the temporary and permanent boundary lines were surveyed, there was no strife amongst them, about their respective possessions, which all were allowed peaceably to hold, until the proper Provincial jurisdiction was established, which was done first, in 1739, by the temporary line, which in the valley, was only half a mile north of the permanent line, established by Mason and Dixon's survey, in 1767. The western boundary, of the same valley, was the Kittochtinny mountains, of seventy miles in extent, being the frontier of the Province, and the Indian claim, extending from that boundary to the far west. The inhabitants of the valley, had for their neighbors, on the frontier, the Indian tribes of the west. Though most of the Indian nations had retired, on the advance of the white settlements, to the western waters, yet, they occasionally, or parts of them, visited the white settlements, for traffic, conference, or to meet other tribes. There was intercourse between them, and the inhabitants of the valley. From the first settlement, in this valley, until the Indians became, with their French allies, the public enemy of the English, and of the inhabitants of their colonies, the life of an Indian was not taken, or the blood of any shed, nor were they deprived of their property, by the inhabitants of this part of the Kittochtinny valley. History, or the public documents, furnish no record of any such wrong to the Indians ; and had there been any such, it would have been made known by the Indians, or by the agents of the Provincial government, who visited them. The Indians, and the inhabitants of this valley, many of whom resided at the base of the Kittochtinny mountain, did maintain an intercourse in peace, and without strife, until 1753, when a hostile spirit was first manifested, under the influence and instigation of the French. Several of the inhabitants of this valley, were carried into captivity, by the Indians, in 1752 and '53. They were subjected to great hardships, by a confinement, for a time, at Quebec, and afterwards in France, where their release was procured by the English Ambassador. On their return to Pennsylvania, the Assembly made provision for their restoration to their homes in the valley. Acts of Assembly, vol. 4.

In September, 1754, a conference was had with the Indians, at the residence of George Croghan, the Indian Agent, at Aughwick. Notwithstanding Mr. Weiser, as the agent of the government, was there, to secure their friendly relations, aided by liberal donations of money; yet, within a few days after, an Indian killed Joseph Campble, a white man, on the Conococheague, near Parnel's Knob, without any known provocation, and made his escape. We have not seen any evidence, documentary, or other, that the inhabitants of this valley were incensed by these repeated outrages of the Indians, at a time of professed peace, to commit against them any acts of revenge, in retaliation for the atrocious wrongs recited, and treacherously perpetrated by the Indians, on the white inhabitants of this valley. In this forbearance, the Scotch Irish race, exhibited a spirit far from being "pugnacious," or that they "hated the Indians," but, that there "were sentiments of honor, or magnanimity in their bosoms, that could restrain resentment."

The success and prosperity of this community, in prosecuting the improvements of their farms, dwelling together in peace, maintaining their social and religious associations, with but the shadow of a public government, is evidence how little government is required for an agricultural people of religious, moral, and industrious habits, content with their occupation. This community, left to their own government, will, we think, for their good habits, bear a comparison with any other population, or any other settlement, of the American colonies, or with any settlement of the lands of the United States, to the same extent.

For fifteen years and more, they lived, with the place of their county offices and sessions of their Courts, at a distance from them, of fifty to one hundred miles ; and when they petitioned the Legislature for the organization of the county of Cumberland, in 1749, they "represented the great hardships they laid under, by being so remote from Lancaster, where the Courts were held, and the public offices kept, and how hard and difficult it was for the 'sober and quiet part' of the people to secure themselves against thefts and other abuses, frequently committed by idle and dissolute persons, who, to escape punishment, resort to the more remote parts of the Province; and owing to the great distance from the Court, or prison, frequently escaped." The obvious necessity, for the relief desired, induced an immediate organization of the county of Cumberland in 1750.

For some time before this, this part of the Kittochtinny valley was called by the whites "the North valley," to distinguish it, we believe, from the extension of the same valley in Virginia, south of the Potomac river. After the organization of Cumberland county, it very generally received the name of the "Cumberland valley," taking its name from the county, of which it was a small part. The Indians, however, long after, in their allusions to it, and the mountain range west, retained their ancient name of "Kittochtinny."

The inhabitants of this valley were destined to experience the sad deficiency, of their Provincial government, in the relations of war. The storm, indicated by the defeat of Braddock, and the dastardly flight of his successor in command, Dunbar, was viewed with terrible apprehension and danger, by the inhabitants along the frontier. These apprehensions were made known, in many memorials to the Assembly and Governor, signed by the mass of the people, imploring immediate measures of defence by the government, for the protection of the settlements exposed. These supplications, acknowledged to be reasonable, and demanding the attention of the government, were not met by legislation, that had any efficiency for the relief of the alarmed inhabitants. The war was allowed to fall on the defenceless inhabitants of this valley, and other settlements, in all the horrors of savage cruelty. Families were surprised in their dwellings, and every member murdered and scalped; their houses and buildings burned, and their cattle destroyed. The men organized themselves into companies, with their own small supply of arms and ammunition, to pursue the enemy, who were generally successful in their rapid retreat to the mountains and the wilderness. This barbarous warfare, was continued for about seven, or more years, against the inhabitants of this valley, who were left, in a great measure, to their own resources and bravery, for the defence of the country against these cruel and powerful enemies. The forts, provided by the government, in the Cumberland valley, at Carlisle, Shippensburg, and Loudon, garrisoned each with about seventy men, afforded little or no protection. Separated by great distances, the Indians, in their incursions, could readily avoid them, as they did, and find still a wide field for an inhuman war, that was regardless of age, sex, or infancy. Even the Royal government, after the defeat of Braddock, in July, 1755, permitted three years and more, to elapse, when in the autumn of 1758, another army, under Gen. Forbes. was marched into the enemy's country, and took possession of Fort Du Quesne, abandoned by the French. So repeated were the massacres of the inhabitants of Cumberland valley, for years, that three fourths of them with their families, sought shelter and safety in the eastern parts of Lancaster and York counties. The men often returned to occupy some dwellings, that escaped the torch of the savage, and coöperate with others, to watch and resist the Indians, whose mode of warfare was secrecy and surprise, murder of the defenceless, and a hasty retreat. The number of white inhabitants, in this valley, slain, scalped, or carried into captivity, was great. The whole extended valley was made one of desolation and blood ; every neighborhood had its victims. The Indian warriors estimated, that in the first years of this war, they killed fifty whites for one Indian that was killed, and in after years, when the white inhabitants better understood their warfare, they still killed ten whites for one of their nation killed by the white inhabitants. This great disproportion arose from the slaughter by the Indians, of women and children, for whose *scalps* their French allies rewarded them liberally.

The distress of the inhabitants of the Cumberland valley, during these wars, may be conceived better than described. Gordon, in his History of Pennsylvania, 383, says: "that incessant anxiety pervaded every family; their slumbers were broken by the yell of demons, or by the dread of an attack, scarce less horrid than an actual attack. The ground was ploughed, the seed sown and the harvest gathered, under the fear of the tomahawk and rifle. Scarcely any outdoor labor was safely executed, unless protected by arms in the hands of the laborers, or by regular troops. Women, visiting their sick neighbors, were shot or captured; children, driving home cattle from the field, were killed and scalped; whilst the enemy dastardly, as well as cruel, shrunk from every equality of force. Many of the richest neighborhoods were deserted, and property of every kind given up to the foe. Many instances of heroism were displayed by men, women and children, in defence of themselves and their homes, and in pursuing and combatting the enemy. There was certainly a great want of ability and energy in the constituted authorities and the government of the Province. United councils, and well directed efforts, might have driven the barbarians to their savage haunts, and repeated the chastisement they received at Kittanning, until they sued for peace. But imbecility distinguished the British ministers and officers, and paralized the efforts of the Provinces, especially that of Pennsylvania."

The complaints against the constituted authorities of the Provincial government, and supplications for defensive measures, were not confined to the Scotch Irish inhabitants of the frontier. The frivolous and endless disputes between the Governor and the Assembly, in a time of war and distress, incensed the German patience and overcame their constitutional "inaction. The inhabitants of the remote parts of Philadelphia county, chiefly Germans, to the amount of four hundred, marched to the city unarmed, in a peaceable and orderly manner, to implore the protection of their rulers, and the postponement of their unreasonable debates. They first waited upon the Governor, who accused the Assembly of procrastination ; and that body did not fail to rebut the charge, whilst they promised their sturdy petitioners, who crowded their hall, that means for their protection and safety should be speedily adopted."*

The Indians were willing to avail themselves of the conciliatory policy of the public authorities, and meet the agents of the Government in conference, when invited ; and in which assurances of peace, friendship and fidelity were given by the Chiefs, who returned to their homes liberally rewarded by presents, at the expense of the government. These pledges and assurances were regarded no longer than the time might be favorable to renew their hostilities on the white inhabitants, who might be surprised in their peaceful occupations, and there barbarously murdered by their false and treacherous foes.

When the treaty of Peace was made, in November, 1762, between the French and English ; and France surrendered its possession in the northern colonies to the English, with the assurances of friendship and peace, received from the Indians, who were so fully represented at a conference with the public agents at Lancaster, in September, in 1762, it was supposed by all interested, that the peace of the Province was established on a basis not to be disturbed.

The inhabitants, who had fled with their families, to the eastern parts of the Province, returned in the autumn of 1762,

---

Gordon, 315.

to the Kittochtinny and adjacent valleys, to resume there the possession of their farms, laid waste by the savage enemy. In the Cumberland valley, the inhabitants, with their characteristic energy, applied themselves to rebuild their dwellings, to procure cattle, and cultivate their lands for a harvest expected to be gathered in safety. All was quiet on the frontiers, not a murmur or threat, from the Indians, that indicated hostility, was heard by the public agents, or by the inhabitants of this valley, who were comforting themselves on the enjoyment of a lasting peace. Sad disappointment was not far from them. "The unprotected state of the frontiers, consequent on the discharge of the forces of the middle and southern colonies, held forth irresistible temptation to the whetted appetite of the border savages for plunder. Their hostility had been rewarded, rather than chastised, by Pennsylvania; every treaty of peace was accompanied by rich presents; and their detention of the prisoners was overlooked, upon slight apologies, though obviously done to afford opportunities for new treaties and additional gift. The mistaken and perverted humanity of 'the Friendly Association,' had softened down their offences."*

A secret and wide spread confederacy among the Indians, was suddenly executed by them, simultaneously, on all the English forts, and the settlements of the frontiers, in the spring and summer of 1763. Their attack on the inhabitants of the Kittochtinny valley, east and west of the Susquehanna, was appalling. "The whole country west of Shippensburg, in this valley, became the prey of the fierce barbarians. They set fire to houses, barns, corn and hay, and every thing that was combustible. The wretched inhabitants, whom they surprised at night, at their meals, or in the labor of the fields, were massacred with the utmost cruelty and barbarity; and those who fled, were scarcely more happy, overwhelmed by sorrow, without shelter, or means of transportation. Their tardy flight was impeded by fainting women and weeping children. The inhabitants of Shippensburg and Carlisle, now became the barrier towns, opened their hearts and houses to their afflicted

* Gordon, 395.

brethren. In the towns, every stable and hovel was crowded with miserable refugees, who, having lost their houses, their cattle and their harvest, were reduced from independence and happiness to beggary and despair. The streets were filled with people, the men distracted, by grief for their losses, and the desire for revenge, more poignantly excited by the disconsolate females and bereaved children who wailed around them."*

The like murders and bloody cruelties were inflicted at the same time, by the barbarous enemy, on the inhabitants of the Kittochtinny valley, east of the Susquehanna. Amongst them, the inhabitants of the township of Paxton, east of where Harrisburg is, in the county of Dauphin, had been sorely afflicted.

The inhabitants, in this district, who had suffered from this inhuman war, were exasperated to excess against the Indians, as a treacherous enemy, on whose stipulations no confidence could be placed, and who were to be intimidated only by a chastisement, that would be an example and terror. Under the influence of these feelings, at a time of great alarm and excitement, attention was directed to the parts of the Delaware and Six Nation tribes, resident on Conestoga, "who refused to join their brethren in arms, professed affection for the colonists, and avowed their determination to remain neutral. That neutrality was denied, and of part of them was very doubtful. Many outrages were committed in consequence, as was generally believed, of the information and advice they gave to the invaders; and some murders were perpetrated, which the public voice ascribed to a party under the protection of the Moravian brethren."†

"That some of the Conestoga Indians were treacherous, appears (says Mr. Rupp) abundantly, from the facts set forth in the affidavits of respectable persons. It was fully believed by the Paxtonians, that what were called the friendly Indians, connived at, if not directly stimulated the hostile ones, in their relentless attacks upon the frontier settlers, at that time."‡ "That these friendly Indians were guilty of treachery and perfidy, in the manor of Conestoga, would seem evident from

* Gordon, 398. † Gordon, 404. ‡ Rupp's His. Lanc., 852–4.

a number of authentic statements and evidence, from other credible sources."*

When the Rev. John Elder, of Paxton, heard that a number of persons had assembled, to proceed to Conestoga, to cut off the Indians, he did all in his power to prevent it. He remonstrated with them on its unlawfulness and barbarity, and assured them that they would be liable to capital punishment. (Letter to Gov. Penn.) His advice and remonstrance were not regarded, and on the 14th Dec., 1763, a number of men from Paxton and Donegal, attacked the Indian village at Conestoga, and there murdered all of the tribe at their town, being six: three men, two women and a boy, and burned their dwellings. Amongst the slain, was one chief, who was distinguished for his friendship to the whites. The majority of the Indians of the town were absent, at the time of the attack. These, by the agents of the Governor and magistrates, were afterwards removed to the jail in Lancaster, as a place of security. Notwithstanding the proclamation of the Governor, offering a reward for the apprehension of the murderers at Conestoga, and enjoining vigilance on the part of the public magistrates, a number of Paxtonians and others, amounting to about thirty persons, suddenly made their appearance in Lancaster, on the 27th day of December, marched to the prison, forced the doors and inhumanly murdered all the Indians found within its walls, regardless of their supplications and protestations of innocence. The number thus murdered were fourteen, three men, three women and eight children."†

Humanity revolts at deeds so cruel and barbarous, as those just recited, only becoming a savage enemy. Cruel as war is, in its mildest forms, it becomes doubly cruel when waged with savages. Their barbarous murder of women, infancy and age, induces in their more intellectual and civilized enemies, revenge and retaliation. It is considered by authorities on national law, that such severities and retaliation, with a ferocious and savage enemy, are legitimate warfare, that by such retaliation they may be brought to a sense of the laws of hu-

* Rupp's His. Dauph., 163. F. vol. 4, Penn. Arch., 139. † Vol. 9, Col. Rec., 103,

manity. It is considered, that by such retaliation only, can Indian barbarities be encountered, and they intimidated. In the wars which the Indians had been waging on the inhabitants of the settlements for seven years, in which most of the victims were women and children, their own families, being remote from the seat of war, escaped, with the exception of the few who fell in the attack on their town of Kittanning, 1756, under the command of Col. Armstrong.

One of the great evils of war, is its corruption of human nature, and hardening the heart to all the sensibilities of humanity. Whilst we condemn the murder of the Conestoga Indians, as atrocious and barbarous, there is some extenuation to be allowed to fathers and husbands, who, but a few months before, were agonized in mourning over murdered wives and children, whose blood, as they firmly believed, was on the hands and skirts of the barbarous and treacherous enemy, who were living near them, under the protection and support of the government. " That inhabitants, whose dwellings had been pillaged and burned, their families murdered and scalped, by an enemy, who, but a few months before, had, in public conference, given the most solemn assurances of peace and friendship, and who renewed their hostilities, without complaint or warning, should be driven to desperation, is not to be wondered at. They were men with the infirmities and passions of men. The desperate combination to avenge on the Conestoga Indians, the barbarous cruelties, inflicted on the border families of the whites, was limited, and confined to a few. The most reliable account on record of them, is to be found in the communication of the Rev. John Elder to Governor Penn, Dec., 16, 1763, who was the pastor of a Presbyterian congregation in the township of Paxton, and who was respected and beloved for his estimable character. Mr. Elder in his letter says: "I thought it my duty to give you this early notice, that an action of this nature may not be imputed to these frontier settlements. For I know not one person of judgment or prudence, that has been in any wise concerned in it ; but it has been done by *some hot-headed, ill-advised persons*, and especially by such, I imagine, as *suffered much in their relations, by the ravages committed by the late Indian war.*"

And in a subsequent letter, from the same, to the Governor, of 27th January, 1764, it is stated, that, "The storm, which had been so long gathering, has at length exploded. Had government removed the Indians from Conestoga, which had frequently been urged without success, this fearful catastrophe might have been avoided. What could I do with men heated to madness? All that I could do was done; I expostulated, but *life* and *reason* were set at defiance, and yet the men in private life, are virtuous and respectable; not cruel, but mild and merciful. The time will come, when each palliating circumstance will be calmly weighed. This deed, magnified into the blackest of crimes, shall be considered as one of those youthful ebullitions of wrath, caused by momentary excitement, to which human infirmity is subjected."

The outrage perpetrated by the murders in the Lancaster jail or work house, was more flagitious, than that at the Indian town. There had been time for passion to subside, and for reason and humanity to resume their control. The doors of a public prison were forced, and the barriers of the law, public faith and security, set at defiance. The authorities of the government, that had the Indians removed to this place, under assurance of protection and safety, were culpable, that they did not, at the peril of their lives, prevent the murderous assassination; or have arrested the perpetrators, in a town having a population of over two thousand, and in it, at the time, a company of the King's troops, under the command of Capt. Robison. Had the magistrates, who assumed the responsibility of protection, repaired to the jail, with a few resolute men, under the panoply of the law, they would have been a host, in themselves, to have repelled the criminal assailants, not numbering more than thirty. Whether successful or not, they were bound by every obligation of duty to have made the attempt, at the hazard of their lives. It is a reflection on the magistrates and authorities, who were instrumental in placing the Indians in the public jail, as well as the citizens of Lancaster, that they permitted this outrage, and the escape of the perpetrators. The insurgents increased in number, by accessions in Lancaster county, and some time after repaired to the neighborhood of Philadelphia, and made threats against the safety of the Indians there, under the protection of the Provincial government. Better councils prevailed with them, and they returned to their homes without any other acts of violence.

The inhabitants of the frontier, who had suffered for so many years, from the ravages of Indian warfare, remained incensed against the Provincial government, which had failed in a first and most imperative duty to its citizens, of protection against a public and savage enemy; and which was feeding and maintaining then, at the public expense, more than one hundred Indians, many of whom were believed by the settlers to have been perpetrators of the most horrid barbarities, but a few months before on the white settlements; and yet the government made no provision for more than a thousand famiilies of the inhabitants of the frontier, reduced to extreme distress, by the destruction of their dwellings, furniture, cattle and crops, and who were dependent on private charity.* They despaired of adequate protection from the government, or a change of the policy of rewarding the Indians by presents, for their promises of good behavior, instead of intimidating them by chastisement,—as long as the government was organized as it was, with its legislature controlled by about one tenth of the population of the Province, who were opposed to military armament, or appropriations for the public defence.

The killing of the Indians at Cònestoga and Lancaster, was aggravated or extenuated by the political parties in Pennsylvania, as they were divided in relation to the administration of the government. We give the representations of that affair, and the public feeling, by the Rev. John Ewing, D. D., who then, and after, sustained a high reputation for learning, intelligence, piety, and purity of character. It is in his letter addressed to Joseph Reed, at London, who was afterwards President of the Executive Council.

Philadelphia, 1764.

"As to public affairs, our Province is greatly involved in intestine feuds, at a time when we should rather unite, one and

---

* Gordon, 408.

all, to manage the affairs of our social government, with prudence and discretion. A few designing men, having engrossed too much power into their hands, are pushing matters beyond all bounds. There are twenty-two Quakers in our Assembly, at present, who, although they wont absolutely refuse to grant money for the King's use, yet never fail to contrive matters in such a manner, as to afford little or no assistance to the poor distressed frontiers; while our public money is lavishly squandered away, in supporting a number of savages, who have been murdering and scalping us for many years past. This has enraged some desperate young men, who had lost their nearest relatives, by these very Indians, to cut off about twenty Indians, that lived near Lancaster, who had, during the war, carried on a constant intercourse with our other enemies; and they came down to Germantown to inquire why Indians, known to be enemies, were supported, even in luxury, with the best that our markets afforded, at the public expense, while they were left in the utmost distress on the frontiers, in want of the necessaries of life. Ample promises were made to them, that their grievances should be redressed, upon which, they immediately dispersed and went home. These persons have been unjustly represented, as endeavoring to overturn the government, when nothing was more distant from their minds. However this matter may be looked upon in Britain, where you know very little of the matter, you may be assured that ninety-nine in an hundred, of the Province, are firmly persuaded, that they are maintaining our enemies, while our friends, who are suffering the greatest extremities, are neglected; and that few, but Quakers, think that the Lancaster Indians have suffered any thing but their just deserts. Tis not a little surprising to us here, that orders should be sent from the Crown to apprehend and bring to justice, those persons who have cut off that nest of enemies, that lived near Lancaster. They never were subjects to his Majesty; were a free, independent State, retaining all the powers of a free State, sat in all our treaties with the Indians, as one of the tribes belonging to the Six Nations, in alliance with us; they entertained the French and Indian spies; gave intelligence to them, of the defenceless state of the Province ; furnished them with our Gazette every week or fortnight; gave them intelligence of all the dispositions of the Province army against them ; were frequently with the French and Indians at their forts and towns ; supplied them with warlike stores; joined with the strange Indians in their war dances, and in the parties that made excursions on our frontiers; were ready to take up the hatchet against the English openly, when the French requested it; actually murdered and scalped some of the frontier inhabitants ; insolently boasted of the murders they had committed, when they saw our blood was cooled, after the last treaty at Lancaster ; confessed that they had been at war with us, and would soon be at war with us again, (which accordingly happened) and even went so far as to put one of their own warriors, Tegarie, to death, because he refused to go to war with them against the English. All these things were known to the frontier inhabitants, and are since proved upon oath. This occasioned them to be cut off by about forty or fifty persons, collected from all the frontier counties, though they are called by the name of the little township of Paxton, where possibly the smallest part of them resided. And what surprises us more than all, the accounts we have from England, is, that our Assembly, in a petition they have drawn up to the King, for a change of government, should represent this Province in a state of uproar and riot, and when not a man in it has once resisted a single officer of the government, nor a single act of violence committed, unless you call the Lancaster affair such, although it was no more than going to war with that tribe, as they had done before with others, without a formal proclamation of war by the government. I have not time, as you may guess, by this scrawl, to write more at this time.

P. S. You may publish the above account, of the Lancaster Indians, if you please."—Life of Reed, Vol. I, page 34.

At this period of excitement, the inhabitants of the frontier and their friends, renewed their accusation against the Quakers, charging them with having encouraged the Indians in their hostilities against the whites, and having aided them when so engaged, with guns and other instruments of death.

These accusations were repelled by them, as unfounded, whilst they reproached the Scotch Irish settlers of the Province, as aiders and abettors of the Conestoga murders, by the party from Paxton. When the charge of cruelty and hatred to the Indian tribes, by the Scotch Irish race, has since been repeated by writers or compilers of history, the evidence to support the allegation, when any was furnished, was a reference to the Conestoga murders. Charges against the Society of Friends, for having encouraged and aided the Indians in their barbarous war on the whites, could only be referred to some few individuals of that respectable class of the population, whose principles were opposed to war, and who were distinguished for peace, order and obedience to the law. It was unreasonable, as well as unjust, to charge either of these large masses of the population of the Province, with the wrongs and crimes perpetrated by a few of their misguided individuals.

On the part of the Scotch and Irish, and the Presbyterian Church, who were implicated by their opponents in these outrages against humanity and law, we repel the imputation as unfounded, and made without evidence and against evidence. There is the authority of the Rev. Mr. Elder, who resided near the residence of these offenders, "that they were a few hot-headed ill-advised persons; that there was not one person of judgment or prudence, that had been in anywise concerned in it." "It was an ebullition of wrath caused by momentary excitement." On these excited men, no person would be supposed to have more influence, than the Rev. Mr. Elder. He was known to have no undue partiality for these Indian enemies, as for years, under the appointment of the Provincial government, he had the command of a company, for the defence of the frontier, against the Indian ravages, which was done faithfully, at the peril of health and life. That influence was exerted in vain, to subdue the excitement, or restrain the desperate purpose of these men. He also dispatched an express after the party of rioters, to inform the government of their hostile purposes. The Governor in his reply to Mr. Elder, dated 29th Dec., 1763, expresses his approbation of his endeavors to prevent the execution of their wicked purposes.

The most extensive and numerous Scotch Irish settlement in the Province, at that time, was in the Cumberland valley, having in it more of the Presbyterian element, dwelling together, than in any other district. It had suffered more from Indian barbarities, than any other part of the Province, and at the time of the murder of the Conestoga Indians, hundreds of its families were mourning over murdered and scalped members, by the hands of treacherous savages; and were destitute of the necessaries of life, of which they had been deprived by the same enemy. The eastern end of this valley was separated from Paxton township only by the river Susquehanna; yet there is no evidence, that the inhabitants of this valley had participated in this transaction, or had any connection with it. There is the highest evidence, from the public documents of the time, to exonerate them from the imputation. Col. John Armstrong, of Cumberland county, at the time a magistrate, and having the command of the Provincial troops of that county, by his letter to Governor Penn, from Carlise, 28th Dec. 1763, acknowledges the receipt of the Governor's proclamation against the offenders at Conestoga, which he had distributed throughout the county, and states: "I have the pleasure to inform your Honor, that not one person of the county of Cumberland, so far as I can learn, has been consulted or concerned in that inhuman and scandalous piece of butchery; and I should be very sorry, that ever the people of this county, should attempt avenging their injuries, on the heads of a few inoffensive and superannuated savages, whom nature had already devoted to the dust."* This is the statement of an intelligent, brave, and honest man, who had the best sources of information, and who would state truly what he did know, without being influenced by fear or favor.

It was this extensive settlement, as before narrated, which maintained, from its commencement, until the Indians became the public enemy, a period of about twenty years friendly and peaceable intercourse with them, without blood-shed, strife or violence.

---

* Penn. Arch. vol. 4, page 152.

We are not aware of any evidence of the Scotch Irish settlers of Bucks, and Chester counties, eastern portion of Lancaster or York counties, as having any connexion with the massacres, perpetrated on the Indians at Conestoga or Lancaster. That they did not discover, or apprehend the perpetrators, if even in their power, was not a criminality that identified them with the offenders. The public mind was then convulsed with excitement and passion, and the public authorities were so unsettled, as to be unsafe holders of the scales of justice. At such a crisis, innocence might readily suffer, and the guilty, escape. The humanity of the law, established as its maxim, that it was better that many guilty persons might escape, than one innocent person suffer wrong, by the adjudication of the law. It allowed not angry passions to direct and control its measures, and impose its penalties. The perpetrators were allowed to escape, by reason of public sentiment being so strong against the Indians, as having been the treacherous and murderous enemy of the frontier inhabitants, and of the unwillingness, on the part of the great majority of the people, to apprehend or punish the men, who had retaliated, as they supposed, on the tribe, some of their bloody cruelties, that had been inflicted on the defenceless white families.

The murder of the Conestoga Indians, with its extenuation, is a stain upon the annals of Pennsylvania. It was a tragedy performed by a few men, under the impulse of feelings excited at the time, by the mangled bodies of wives and children on the frontier, from the hands of Indians, in which the Conestoga Indians, if not active participants, were believed to be aiders and abettors. The reproach of this single act of barbarous warfare, is not to be put down to the condemnation of Pennsylvania, or any classes of her inhabitants, or to subject them to the charge of excess against humanity.

Reproachful as this warfare was to the Province, it is to be recollected, that Pennsylvania, was not the only colony of North America, which, in times of excitement, had allowed high crimes to be perpetrated with impunity, under less extenuating circumstances in their early governments, by excesses and outrages against the law and the lives and the property of their people. Massachusetts had its judicial murders, in the tribunals of the law, by trials conducted in the usual form, by which innocent men and women in numbers were convicted and executed for witchcraft. The city of New York, in 1741, with a population of about eight thousand, was the theatre of a cruel and bloody delusion, not less lamentable, under which judges and lawyers prostituted their stations, to sacrifice under color of law, slaves falsely accused of arson—tried without counsel—convicted upon insufficient evidence—and of whom *thirteen were burned at the stake*, eighteen hanged, and seventy one transported.*

At the recital of such tragedies, humanity revolts, and deplores the infirmity and depravity that perpetrated them, as well as the weakness of the law, and the inefficiency of its constituted authorities, that allowed the escape of the offenders with impunity.

Lawless and riotous proceedings were had near Fort Loudon in March 1765, in which some of the inhabitants of Cumberland valley, residing near the base of the Kittochtinny mountain, participated. It being known that a large amount of goods had been brought into the neighborhood, from Philadelphia, in wagons, to be carried by the Indian traders on pack horses to places of Indian trade, in and west of the mountains, a party of men assembled, amounting to about fifty, where Mercersburg is now situated, being on the traders' road. They there met the traders with their horses and goods on the way. One of the assembled party, Mr. Duffield, who was respected and prominent in the county, desired the persons having charge of the horses and goods, to store them and not proceed without further orders. They made light of this request and disregarded it, by pursuing their way over the mountain to the west. The assembled party pursued them across the Tuscarora mountain into the Great Cove, and again urged them to store up their goods. Mr. Duffield reasoned with them, on the impropriety of their proceedings, and the great danger the frontier inhabitants would be exposed to, if the Indians should now get

* Hil. His., Vol. 2, p. 392.

a supply, as it was well known they had scarcely any ammunition. To supply them now, would be a kind of murder, and would be illegally trading at the expense of the blood and safety of the frontiers. The traders ridiculed what he said, and disregarded it. Mr. Duffield and his party returned to their homes, without any attempt to restrain the trading party. Lieut. James Smith, one of Mr. Duffield's party, was not satisfied to be so repulsed. Mr. Smith had commanded, for some years, a company of Rangers, employed in the defence of that frontier, against the incursions of the savages. He was a man of resolution, of indomitable courage, and inflexible from any purpose which he deemed necessary, for the safety of the inhabitants. With *ten* of his old company, he, the following night, pursued the traders, whom they overtook on Sideling Hill. They attacked them by shooting their horses, and required them to leave their goods, except their private property, and retire. This was done, and the goods for trading, consisting, amongst other things, of blankets, lead, tomahawks and scalping knives, were burned and destroyed, and after this, gun powder, which they had stored. The traders, returned to Fort Loudon, which was then under the command of Lieut. Grant, a Royal officer, with a company of Highland soldiers. The Lieutenant assigned to them a guard of soldiers, who assisted in arresting, without oath, warrant, or any process from a magistrate, a number of the inhabitants of the neighborhood, who had no concern in the attack on the traders, or the destruction of their goods, and who were brought to Fort Loudon and there confined. Smith soon appeared before the Fort, with three hundred riflemen under his command, when a parley was had, which led to the immediate release of the confined inhabitants. There was still kept in the Fort some of their guns, that had been taken by the soldiers. Lieut. Grant, having gone into the country, near the Fort, was taken into custody by some of the dissatisfied inhabitants, and released on his promise to deliver up the guns withheld in the Fort, and which was complied with.

The author of these violent proceedings was Lieut. Smith, having with him ten of his rangers. The inhabitants of the neighborhood of Fort Loudon promptly assembled to resist and redress the arbitrary and illegal proceedings of the soldiers from Fort Loudon, in arresting and confining at their will, respectable persons who had no participation in the affair. The proceedings of Smith, and his party, had their approbation, as necessary to the defence and safety of that frontier against a savage enemy. That enemy had the preceding summer, surprised the inhabitants of Conococheague, by their sudden and unexpected attack, inflicted on them the most cruel barbarities, murdering and scalping many, amongst whom, was a schoolmaster, and the children of the school. Several tribes of Indians were still in hostile attitude in their wild retreats, on the western waters. As the government had no force adequate to the protection of the frontier; or the chastisement of the skulking and bloody savages, who were generally successful in their ravages, the great reliance for peace on the frontier, was the want of means and supplies with the Indians, to enable or encourage them to renew their murderous incursions.

An Act of Assembly of Oct., 1763, prohibited the selling of guns, powder, or other warlike stores, to the Indians. The trader, who had a license to trade with the Indians, was prohibited from selling them military stores, or war implements. These traders had long been reputed, vicious, lawless and profligate, regardless of the law, the Governor's proclamations and the complaints of the Indians, in relation to their traffic with the Indians in *Rum*. The provincial government acknowledged its inability to restrain them, and execute the law; and advised the Indians before the Indian wars, to execute the law themselves against the traders, by seizing and destroying the Rum brought to their trading places. The government had not yet done any thing efficient, for the defence of the frontier inhabitants. Those in the Cumberland valley, had been left, in a great measure, to their own resources and defences, during the nine years of Indian war, following Braddock's defeat. To them, these wars were attended with the sacrifice of many men, women and children, and the destruction of much of their property.

The apprehension of the renewal of these savage wars in the

coming season, was overwhelming to the inhabitants on west Conococheague, who, living near the base of the mountains, through which the Indians had their war paths, were most exposed to their incursions. That apprehension was well founded, and the danger imminent, if the Indians were stimulated by a supply from the traders of military stores and implements of murder. The public exigency and safety demanded prompt action; the peace of the country was involved. The question was one of life or death, to an extensive settlement. The only effectual restraint upon them, and others pursuing the same trade, was the destruction of their property. This, weighed against the blood, lives and property of the inhabitants of this frontier, was as the dust of the balance. The men, who had for years periled their lives in defence of that frontier, assumed to seize and destroy their military stores, on their way to the enemy.

The proceedings of these border inhabitants against the Indian traders and the garrison at Fort Loudon, were very offensive to the officers of government. Gen. Gage, who commanded the Royal forces in the Province, was indignant at the disrespect manifested for the King's fort and garrison. The Governor had warrants issued for the arrest of Lieut. Smith, and the other offenders.

The public sentiment, of the great mass of the people, was so manifest, in favor of the arbitrary proceedings of Smith and his friends, as necessary to the public defence and safety of human lives, that the criminal proceedings instituted against them were withdrawn; and as a treaty of peace was formed shortly after the occurrence, with the remaining tribes of Indians, who had been hostile, the public fears were allayed, and the traders pursued their traffic, having more regard to the laws and public opinion.

In the year 1768, there was a riotous and lawless proceeding, by a party of rioters, in rescuing from the prison in Carlisle, Frederick Stump, a German, with his German servant man, who were in confinement on the charge of murdering in Sherman's valley, west of the Kittochtinny mountain, ten Indians: four men, three women and three children. Of their guilt, there was no doubt. The murder was unprovoked, and indefensible, and in defence of himself, the monster only alleged that the Indians were intoxicated and disorderly, and he apprehended some injury. Some of his indignant neighbors arrested him and his servant, and lodged them in Carlisle jail. A warrant had been issued by the Chief Justice of the Province for the arrest of Stump, and required him to be brought before him at Philadelphia, "to answer for said murders, and to be dealt with according to law."* Though public opinion was strong against the prisoners, that they ought to be convicted and punished, with all the severity of the law, yet the warrant for the removal of Stump to Philadelphia, was considered an illegal encroachment on the rights of the citizen, who, by law, was secured a trial for his crime in the county where committed, and a jury of the vicinage for his triers, and that the removal of Stump, if allowed, might be a precedent for the removal of innocent men, who might be oppressed by a trial in a distant jurisdiction. Opposition to his removal was expressed and threats were made, inducing an apprehension of rescue from the Sheriff, on his way to Philadelphia, if attempted. It would seem that a regard to the law, public justice and the safe keeping of the prisoner, as well as to quiet the minds of the people, induced Justice Armstrong, with some other magistrates, to confer on the subject, and after executing a commitment of Stump to the jail, on the charge of murder, they advised the Sheriff, for fear of rescue on the way, which was threatened, until further orders were received from the government, to defer the removal. A party under arms, who had assembled for the rescue, then dispersed, when informed that Stump and his servant man were committed to the jail of Cumberland.

Two days after, an armed party of Stump's friends from Sherman's valley came to Carlisle, and being joined by some others, amounting to about seventy, at an early hour in the day, approached the jail with arms, having sent a few without arms before them, who were admitted within the door

* Col. Rec., Vol. 9, p. 416.

of the jail. Col. Armstrong, with some other magistrates and citizens, on the first alarm, repaired to the jail, and there expostulated with the rioters and commanded them to desist from their unlawful purpose of rescuing the prisoners. Whilst Justice Armstrong was striving to disperse them, the rioters disregarded the magistrates, and repelled them with indignities and violence, and by numbers and arms effected the rescue of Stump and Ironsetter, whom they carried off in the direction of the mountains.* Carlisle was then but a small village, with a population too few to repel, or arrest the armed rioters, whose lawless act at the jail was a surprise, and occupied but a few minutes. The rioters were immediately pursued by Col. Armstrong, the Sheriff, Rev. Mr. Steele, and others, who hoped to be able to induce them to return the prisoners, but did not overtake them. The rioters, apprehensive of pursuit, hastened across the mountain to Sherman's valley. The magistrates, in person, with the sheriff, proceeded in a day or two after, into Sherman's valley, in search of the prisoners and their party, but without success. Stump had fled, it was said, to Lancaster county, where his relatives resided, having his German servant with him. From that, it was believed, they made their escape into Virginia, and of them no further intelligence was heard, though the Governor of Pennsylvania offered a reward of £200 for the apprehension of Stump and £100 for the apprehension of Ironsetter.

Gov. Penn, in his letter to Col. Armstrong, dated 3rd Feb., 1768, reproves the magistrates of Cumberland county, for their "insolence, who had taken upon them to suggest, or even to suppose, that the government or judges intended to do so illegal an act, as to try the prisoners in any other county or place than where the fact was committed," and that he was to be removed to the city only for *examination.*† The magistrates and inhabitants of Cumberland county, were excusable, for not comprehending why these criminals were to be conveyed to the city of Philadelphia, with a guard and at the risk of escape or rescue, for the mere purpose of examination, to be reconveyed

* Col. Rec., Vol. 9, 450–462–464–484.

† Col. Rec., Vol. 9, 446.

to Carlisle for trial, when the crime of murder, with which they were charged, was admitted by them, on which they were committed to the county prison at Carlisle, by the magistrates of Cumberland, having authority, where they were in confinement and in irons, to await their trial.

In a communication from Col. Armstrong to the Governor, of 7th Feb., 1768, he says: "I assure you, after the closest examination I have been able to make, even the ignorant and giddy crowd who have committed this hasty, flagrant violation of the established course of justice, have done it under the mistaken apprehension of the intention of carrying Stump to Philadelphia."* Though the feeling of the mass of the people was indignation towards these barbarous murderers, yet they were not satisfied that a precedent should be established in a case so criminal, that might be used again to the prejudice of others, unjustly accused. The friends of Stump, who were desirous of his escape, took advantage of the general feeling in the county, against the illegality of the removal of the prisoners, and with the assistance of some of these persons, were successful in effecting the rescue of Stump. Their offence was a great one against public justice, to be reprobated by every good citizen. Such offences, if allowed to pass without signal punishment, impair the structure of government and endanger the security and safety of the community, and lessen the respect for the public authorities and law, in substituting anarchy and violence for law and peace. It was a great reflection on the magistrates of Cumberland county, and its inhabitants, that these two savage white men should have been allowed to escape the severest penalty of the law, which they deserved.

This riotous act is not to be imputed to any one national class or religious denomination. It was made up of persons professing to belong to several. Justices Armstrong, R. Miller, W. Lyon, Rev. Mr. Steele, and others, who were active and resolute in opposing the rioters, as well as pursuing them and the prisoners, were of Irish nativity, and belonged to the Presbyterian Church. Though Stump and Ironsetter were Germans

* Col. Rec., Vol. 9, 462.

and may have been assisted in their rescue and escape, by some of their German relatives; it would be unjust and illiberal, to reproach the German population of Cumberland or Lancaster counties, for the crimes of these reckless individuals.

The Kittochtinny valley, east and west of the Susquehanna, being, during the Indian wars, the frontier of the Province of Pennsylvania, was harassed for eight years and more, with all the ravages and cruelties of savage warfare. The defence of it was cast almost entirely on the inhabitants, by the remissness of the Royal and Provincial governments, to provide for the public defence ; men would organize themselves into military companies, under the command of some selected leader. Amongst the first companies organized on west Conococheague, on the bloody outbreak by the Delaware Indians, in 1755, was one, which selected for its captain, the Rev. John Steele, their Presbyterian pastor. This command was accepted by Mr. Steele, and executed with so much skill, bravery and judgment, as to commend him to the Provincial government, which appointed him a Captain of the Provincial troops. This appointment he retained for many years, to the benefit of the public service and the satisfaction of the government. He was reputed a sound divine, of piety and learning, and did not relinquish the ministry for arms. Such was the state of the country, that he often exercised his ministry with his gun at his side, addressing his congregation, the men of which, had their weapons within their reach.

One of the most efficient men of that day, in the Cumberland valley, was Col. John Armstrong of Carlisle, of Irish nativity, and an elder in the Presbyterian Church. He was a man of intelligence, of integrity and of high religious and moral character. He was resolute and brave, and though living habitually in the fear of the Lord, he feared not the face of man.

Dr. Hugh Mercer, a Scotchman, of talent and education, had taken up his residence in the southern part of this valley, near the Maryland line, a short time before Braddock's defeat. Having enjoyed some military training and experience in Europe, and having a taste for military life, he was early in 1756, appointed a Captain in the Provincial service, in which he was continued for some years, being promoted to the rank of Colonel.

Col. Armstrong and Col. Mercer were, in 1776, appointed by the American Congress, Generals of its Revolutionary Army, on the recommendation of Washington, who had served with them in Forbes' campaign in 1758, and knew their qualifications. Col. Armstrong served his country with ability and fidelity in the trying struggle for American Independence. General Mercer, highly esteemed by Washington, and having the confidence of the army and the country, fell, mortally wounded and mangled, by the British soldiery, at the battle of Princeton, in January, 1777, whilst gallantly and bravely leading his division against the royal army.

There might be named many other officers, who rendered signal services, as commanders of Provincial troops, or of rangers, in the Kittochtinny valley, during the Indian wars, exposing their health and lives in defence of their country and friends.

The expedition organized by Col. Armstrong, in this valley, in 1756, for an attack on the Indian town and fortress at Kittaning, west of the mountains, was conducted, through a mountainous country in the possession of the enemy, with a skill, judgment, celerity, bravery, hardihood and success, not surpassed by any armament, or other military expedition of the Colonies. The corporation of Philadelphia, on this victory, addressed a complimentary letter to Colonel Armstrong, thanking him and his officers, for their gallant conduct, and presented to him a piece of plate, and a medal, struck for the occasion, with a suitable device.

During these wars, more than half of the inhabitants of the Cumberland valley sought safety for themselves and families in the eastern parts of York and Lancaster counties. Pastors could no longer assemble their congregations for worship, without great peril, and for security, they accompanied their friends to the older settlements. Even the schools had to be discontinued ; for the master and scholars of a school in the very heart of the Conococheague settlement, were barbarously murdered by a party of Indians, who had penetrated the valley without discovery, and when their hostilities were not apprehended. A classical school had been established by Mr. John King, (afterwards the Rev. Dr. King) in the year 1761, in the Conococheague settlement, which was continued for some years, until the incursions of the savages made it unsafe.

In and after 1765, the inhabitants, who had fled, returned with their familes to the valley, resumed their desolate and dilapidated farms; applied themselves with renewed industry and perseverance, to re-build dwellings, prepare their fields for a crop of grain, and replenish their furniture and stock of cattle and farm implements, as fast as resources and opportunities would allow. Congregations were assembled for worship, as in the preceding times of peace, and in 1767–69, pastors were again called to, and installed over the several Presbyterian congregations in the valley, vacated by the wars and ravages of a barbarous enemy. Several of these, Dr. Cooper, Dr. King, and Dr. Duffield, were men eminent for learning, piety, and usefulness in the Presbyterian Church.

The settlement progressed rapidly in population and improvement. The only public grievances commanding attention, for some years, were political ones, common to the inhabitants of this Province and of the other colonies, who, in public and private, discussed the relations between the colonies and parent State, involving the constitutional and chartered rights of American freemen. The Irish and Scotch emigrants, who had removed from the mother country and friends, to cross the ocean for a wilderness, were not subjects for passive obedience; or willing to surrender their rights or liberties to the exactions of either King or Parliament.

CHAPTER IV.

The Scotch Irish opposition to British taxation—Kittochtinny or Cumberland valley, in favor of American Independence——Resolutions—-Military organizations—-Early expression of public sentiment in favor of separation from Great Britain—Participation in maintenance of Independence—Prompt action to form an army— Congress of 1776 *—Irish and Scotch members from Pennsylvania—Abilities—Influence and measures—After war, inhabitants of Cumberland county resumed their labors on their farms—Regard for Education—Dickinson College.*

WHEN the wrath of the Royal government was poured out on the colony of Massachusetts, and the port of Boston closed, there was no class in any of the colonies, with whom there was greater sympathy, for the oppressed of New England, or who were more indignant against the tyrannical measures of the Royal government, than with the Irish and Scotch inhabitants of Pennsylvania, and their immediate descendants.

At a meeting of the freeholders and freemen of Cumberland county, held at Carlisle on the 12th of July, 1774, John Montgomery, Esq., of Irish nativity, in the Chair, resolutions were adopted in condemnation of the act of Parliament closing the port of Boston, and recommending vigorous and prudent measures to obtain a redress of grievances. They recommended a general Congress of deputies from all the colonies—the non-importation of any merchandize from Great Britain, or dependencies, and promised contributions to the relief of their suffering brethren in Boston. At this meeting, deputies were appointed to meet, immediataly, others from other counties of the Province, at Philadelphia, to concert measures preparatory to the general Congress. Their deputies were James Wilson, of Scotch nativity, a member of the Congress of 1776, a signer of the Declaration of Independence; and after the organization of the Federal government, a Judge of the Supreme Court of the United States,—William Irwin and Robert Magaw, of Irish origin, the first of whom, was a General, and the latter, a Colonel, in the army of the Revolution, from Pennsylvania.

The blood of American freeman was first shed at Lexington by British soldiery, under the command of their Royal officers, on the 19th April 1775, and proclaimed, that the arbitrary acts of parliament and the tyrannical measures of the ministry, were to be enforced by arms. The intelligence in Pennsylvania was received with a blaze of indignation. Though war news, in those days, were only transmitted with the speed of the post horse, and there were only six or eight newspapers published in the Province, yet the tocsin of alarm soon extended through its towns, villages, hills and valleys. At Philadelphia, on the 24th of April, its citizens assembled in thousands, resolved to form military associations for the protection of their property, liberties and lives. The like associations were immediately formed in the adjoining counties. In the distant county of Cumberland, the war cry was no sooner sounded, than its freemen rallied in thousands, for military association and organization, in defence of their rights. The American archives preserve a letter from Carlisle, written on 6th May, 1775, in which it is stated: "Yesterday the County committee met from nineteen townships, on the short notice they had. Above three thousand men have already associated, the arms returned amounted to about fifteen hundred. The committee have voted five hundred effective men, besides commissioned officers, to be immediately drafted, taken into pay, armed and disciplined to march on the first emergency, to be paid and supported as long as necessary, by a tax on all estates, real and personal, in the county."* This was not vapor on the part of the men of Cumberland valley. They were sincere and in earnest in their associations, and inflexible in purpose, as a short time evinced. The memorable engagement

* Amer. Arch., Vol. 2, 516.

at Breed's and Bunker's Hill, on the 17th of June, 1775, aroused the colonists to increased activity. It proved that untrained militia could contend successfully with trained and disciplined veterans; and whilst it astounded British commanders, it increased the confidence of the American patriot, in the safety of his liberty and rights. The sword was drawn by both contending parties, and their measures were for battle; negotiation and concession were no longer to be allowed to subjects, by a haughty and tyrannical government. The controversy was to be settled by the last resort of nations—arms. The colonists saw before them a protracted war, with all its calamities, between which, and abject submission, they had no alternative. They chose the former, regardless of its cost and sacrifices. The Royal commanders, with their ministerial rulers, anticipated but a single campaign, in which their trained and well provided army was to march where it pleased to subdue and punish the flying rebels.

The public service and defence of the country, demanded from the colonies, an army adequate to the emergency. Congress, in May, 1775, in apportioning that army, required from Pennsylvania four thousand three hundred men. The appointment of Washington, by the unanimous vote of the Continental Congress, as Commander in Chief of their army, was in itself, a tower of strength to the colonists.

The military spirit and ardor of the freemen of Pennsylvania, were not abated, by the prospect of immediate service in the American army, in a distant colony.

The call for a military force was responded to from the city of Philadelphia, and the inland counties, with great alacrity, and by immediate measures of organization and preparation. The freemen of this Province did not wait for forced draughts; companies of volunteers were immediately organized, to be commanded by officers of their own choice. From the Cumberland valley, in the summer of 1775, companies, under the command of officers of their choice, obeyed from inclination and respect, marched to join the army under the command of Washington, in the seige of Boston. One of these companies was from Chambersburg, under the command of James Chambers, as Captain, which marched in June, 1775, and joined the army at Boston, in August, 1775, under the command of Washington. James Chambers being in a short time advanced to the rank of a Colonel of the regular army, remained in the military service of the country till the close of the Revolutionary war.

Other companies were from west Conococheague, Shippensburg, Carlisle and the eastern part of the county. These were made up of many hardy and efficient men, the heads of families, respectable and substantial freeholders. They were without acquaintance with the discipline of European armies, and without military dress, or accoutrements. They were all familiar with the use of fire arms, and some had experience in the frontier wars against the French and Indians. They were the men for the times, inured to toil and exposure; stout and athletic. They were soldiers, who could march, when an emergency required, without tents or baggage wagons, carrying their equipments in their knapsacks. With a blanket they could sleep on the bare earth, with the open air for their apartment, and the firmament for their covering. The campaign of these men was not a mere parade, or a summer excursion, to see the enemy and return to their homes. An extended service was before them, not to be mistaken, and many of these men are known to have remained from that time, in the military service of their country for years, and some of them until Independence was acknowledged and the army disbanded; having only at distant intervals, made a short visit to their families when the public service would allow. Some others had, in other colonies, a soldier's burial and grave.

Notwithstanding the bloody contest with arms, in which the colonists were now engaged, in defence of their lives, liberties, and properties, against the armies of the Royal government, there was still manifested universally a repugnance to dissolve the connection between the colonists and the parent State. The Assembly of Pennsylvania, in the appointment of delegates, in November, 1775, to represent the Province in Congress, expressly instructed them, "that you, in behalf of this colony, dissent from and utterly reject, any propositions, should such be made, that may cause, or lead to *a separation* from our mother country, or a change of the form of this government."*

The progress of the war and the oppressive exactions of the British government, after a few months unsettled public opinion on this question, and the necessity and policy of independence, became a debatable question with the colonists, in their social meetings. At this time there was no newspaper published in Pennsylvania, we believe, west of York. The freemen of the county of Cumberland, in this Province, were amongst the first to form the opinion, that the safety and welfare of the colonies, did render separation, from the mother country, necessary. The first public expression of that sentiment, and its embodiment in a memorial, emanated from the freemen and inhabitants of that county, to the Assembly of the Province, and is amongst the national archives.† It is an able, temperate, patriotic expression of the considerations that induced them to petition the Assembly, "that the last instructions which it gave to the delegates of this Province in Congress, wherein they are enjoined not to consent to any step which may cause or lead to a separation from Great Britain, *may be withdrawn*." This memorial was presented to the Assembly on the 28th of May, 1776, and on the 5th of June, after a debate of considerable length, was referred, by a large majority, to a committee, to bring in new instructions to the delegates of this Province in Congress.‡ Instructions, in conformity to the memorial of the Province of Cumberland, were reported, adopted, and signed by the Speaker, June 14th, wherein it is stated: "The situation of public affairs is since (their instructions of November) so greatly altered, that we now think ourselves justifiable in removing the restrictions laid upon you by those instructions."§ The memorial from Cumberland county bears evidence that the inhabitants of that county were in advance of their representatives in the Assembly, and in Congress, on the subject of Independence. The considerations suggested by them, had their influence on the Assembly, who adopted the

* Amer. Arch. Vol. 3, 1408. † Amer. Arch., 4th series, Vol. 5, 850-1. ‡ Ib. 858. § Ib. 862.

petition of the memorialists, and *withdrew* the instructions that had been given to the delegates in Congress, in opposition to Independence. As the Cumberland memorial was presented to the Assembly on the 23rd of May, 1776, it probably had occupied the attention and consideration of the inhabitants of the Cumberland valley, early in that month. As there was no remonstrance from this district, by any dissatisfied with the purposes of the memorial, we are to suppose, that it expressed the public sentiment of that large, respectable, and influential district of the Province, which had then many officers and men in the ranks of the Continental army.

Resolutions, in favor of Independence, were adopted by the citizens of Mecklenberg county, North Carolina, on the 20th of May, 1775. But the feeling there, at that time, was by no means general; and counter combinations were also entered into for sustaining the royal authority.

The Virginia convention, on the 15th of May, 1776, instructed the Virginia delegates in Congress, to propose to that body a Declaration of Independence. In obedience to this, Richard H. Lee, of Virginia, submitted to Congress, on the 7th of June, the resolution, "That the United Colonies, are, and ought to be, free and independent States, and that their political connection with Great Britain, is, and ought to be, dissolved."* This resolution, after much debate, was passed, on the 8th, by a bare majority, seven States to six, the delegates of Pennsylvania, New Jersey and Maryland, being expressly instructed against it. The subject was postponed till the first of July, and a committee appointed to prepare a formal declaration of independence. The outside influence of the freemen, as well as of other public assemblies, in Pennsylvania, were in favor of independence. The Provincial Conference of Pennsylvania assembled at Philadelphia, of which Thomas McKean was President, unanimously, on the 24th of June, declared "their willingness to concur in a vote of the Congress, declaring the United Colonies free and independent States," which was signed and presented to Congress.† The sense of the military in

* Hild. U. S., Vol. 3, 74. † Am. Arch., Vol. 5, 962.

the rank, from Pennsylvania, then in the neighborhood of Philadelphia, were taken by their commanders, on this momentous question. When the question was submitted to Col. McKean's battalion of four hundred, on the 10th of June, it was carried unanimously in the affirmative, and their approbation manifested by three huzzas. In other battalions, at the same time, resolutions were adopted unanimously, disapproving of the instructions of the Assembly of Pennsylvania to the delegates in Congress, restricting them in their action. The Assembly of Pennsylvania, as before stated, yielding to the expression of public sentiment, by the freemen of Cumberland valley, as well as by the Pennsylvania forces, in the army, who were staking their lives on the issue, with arms in their hands, on the side of independence, on the 14th of June *rescinded* their instructions to the delegates in Congress, who were at liberty to vote on the question of independence, untrammelled by the instructions of November.

The committee having reported, a formal Declaration of Independence, which, with the resolution on the subject, was brought up in Congress on the 1st of July ; the majority of the Pennsylvania delegates, remained inflexible in their unwillingness to vote for the measure, at the head of which opposition was the distinguished patriot, John Dickinson, who opposed the measure, not as bad, or uncalled for, but as premature. But when, on the 4th of July, the subject came up for final action, two of the Pennsylvania delegates, Dickinson and Morris, who had voted in the negative, absented themselves, and the vote of Pennsylvania was carried by the votes of Franklin,* Wilson and Morton, against the votes of Willing

* "Franklin had been made to feel, in the city of Philadelphia, in 1764, the uncertainty of popular favor, and the power of party prejudice, by a defeat in his election to the Assembly, after having been chosen for fourteen years successively. This was an empty triumph to his opponents, as the Assembly who convened, by a large majority, appointed him special agent to the Court of Great Britain, to carry out the purpose of a change of Provincial government and to manage the general affairs of the Province. John Dickinson, who opposed this appointment, and inveighed strenuously against the *political principles* and conduct of Franklin, eulogized him as a man. The power of party and prejudice separated, for a time, these two statesmen and patriots, and distorted truth and perverted judgment. Franklin was more than restored to public confidence. He was the advocate and signer of the Declaration of Independence, and amongst those who refused to affix his

and Humphreys. The men who voted in opposition to this measure, were esteemed honest and patriotic men, but were too timid for the crisis. They faltered and shrunk from responsibility and danger, when they should have been firm and brave. The convention of Pennsylvania at once recalled its quaking delegates, and elected in their places, Colonels George Ross, James Smith, Dr. Benjamin Rush, George Clymer and George Taylor. Though the Declaration of Independence was adopted on the 4th of July, it was not signed until the 2nd of August, 1776, when the new delegates from Pennsylvania were present, and affixed their names to it. The convention selected the majority of the new delegates from the interior of the Province: Col. Ross, from Lancaster, Col. Smith, from York, and George Taylor, from Northampton, James Wilson, being then from Cumberland. Mr. Wilson, as has been stated, was of Scotch nativity, whilst Col. Smith and Mr. Taylor were Irishmen, all of whom had long been in the Province and identified with its best interests, and were ready to jeopard all that was dear to them, in defence of the liberties and indepennence of their adopted country. Amongst the other signers of the Declaration of Independence, were a number of Scotch or Irish nativity, or their immediate descendants.

The spirit of the Presbyterian ministers, on the side of American Independence, was exemplified by the Rev. John Witherspoon, D. D., and LL. D., President of Princeton College, of Scotch nativity and education, and eminent for talents, learning and eloquence. He was a member of Congress when the Declaration of Independence was reported, and was before the House for the signature of its members. Some seemed to waver, and deep and solemn silence reigned throughout the Hall. This venerable man, casting on the assembly a look of inexpressible interest, and unconquerable determination, remarked: "That noble instrument on your table, which insures immortality to its author, should be subscribed this

---

name to this instrument, was the virtuous, patriotic, able, but irresolute John Dickinson. This want of firmness, at this crisis, turned the tide of public sentiment, for a time, against him, whilst Franklin was elevated to the highest place in public estimation."

very morning by every pen in the House. He, who will not respond to its accents, and strain every nerve to carry into effect its provisions, is unworthy the name of a freeman. Although these gray hairs must descend into the sepulchre, I would infinitely rather they should descend thither by the hand of the public executioner, than desert at this crisis, the sacred cause of my country. The patriarch sat down, and forthwith the Declaration was signed by every member present." [Rev. S. S. Templeton.]

By the Declaration of Independence, the Rubicon was passed. There was no way of honorable retreat, or door open for safe reconciliation. The prospect before the American freemen was a struggle that was awfully fearful. The contest was one of liberty and life, against death or subjection. There were no half way measures. It was for every American to choose which side he would take, whether on the side of American liberty and independence, or that of a royal and despotic master. Some faltered, were undecided and watched to know the end of the terrible beginning. Others, who had been basking in royal favor, or whose associations had been with men in high places, joined the enemy, and were proclaimed traitors under a load of infamy, they could never remove from their characters.

Men and arms were now required to fill up and strengthen the American army, which was sadly reduced, and was both imperfectly equipped and scantily provided. To supply the deficiency, Congress, whilst Independence was in agitation before them, called for, from Pennsylvania, Delaware and Maryland ten thousand men, of which Pennsylvania was to furnish six thousand, to constitute a flying camp for the protection of New Jersey. At the same time, a requisition of near fourteen thousand more were required from New England, New York, and New Jersey, for the general defence.

The spirit in Pennsylvania that induced the Declaration of Independence ,was no less vigorous after that responsible act. It did not evaporate in memorials, resolutions or speeches, but buckled on its armor to meet the enemies of the country. From the eastern and interior portions of the Province, the requisition of Congress was promptly met, by their men in arms, in companies, battalions and regiments. The Scotch Irish settlements were at once thinned of their brave, hardy and patriotic freemen. To notice their divisions, commanders and numbers, would extend too much our remarks for this article. The Cumberland valley, though more remote, and not free from Indian alarm, occasioned by savage incursions, through the western mountains, into the adjoining county of Bedford, then having but a small and sparse population, with an alacrity to be admired, furnished its volunteers, in companies, under the command of officers of their choice, ready to obey the commands of their country, in whatever battle field, or post of danger to which they might be called. In a letter from the committee of Cumberland county to the President of Congress, dated at Carlisle, July 14th, 1776, it is stated : "By the intelligence we have already received, we think ourselves warranted to say, that we shall be able to send *five* companies, viz : one from each battalion, to compose part of the flying camp, provided so many good arms can be had, and three companies of militia for the present emergency, some of whom will march this week. With pleasure, we assure you, that a noble spirit appears amongst the inhabitants here. The spirit of marching to the defence of our country, is so prevalent in this town, that we shall not have men left sufficient to mount guard, which we think absolutely necessary for the safety of the inhabitants and ammunition, and as a watch over the ten *English* officers, with their ten servants, to keep their patrol of honor, especially as their brethren, lately, at Lebanon, in Lancaster county, lost it; and as there will not be more left in town for the above purpose, we shall be obliged to hire a guard of twelve men from the county."*

In a letter, from the same committee, to Congress, dated at Carlisle, July 31st, 1776, it is said : "The inhabitants have voluntarily and very generally offered their services, and by the answers which we have received from the officers, it appears to us that *eleven* companies will be sufficiently armed and ac-

---

* Amer. Arch., 5 Ser., 1 Vol., p. 328.

coutred, and the last of them marched from this place in about a week from this time. Three companies more are preparing if they can get arms, and many more declare themselves willing to march; but we are well assured, arms are not to be got in this county. If arms and accoutrements are to be had at Philadelphia, we can send *more men*."*

In a letter, from the same committee, to Congress, from Carlisle, dated August 16th, 1776, it is stated, that "The *twelfth* company of our militia are marched to day, which companies contain, in the whole, eight hundred and thirty-three privates, with officers, nearly nine hundred men. Six companies more are collecting arms, and are preparing to march."† ‡

At the time these volunteers, from the Cumberland valley, were pressing forward, in surprising numbers, it is to be recollected, that from this district, there were then in the Continental army a number of officers, as well as rank and file, who, the year preceding, had entered the army, and were still absent in the military service of their country.

Was there anywhere, in the colonies, more patriotism, resolution, and bravery, that was thus evinced, on a call to arms, than by the hardy, intelligent citizen soldiers of this Scotch Irish settlement. Their territory and dwellings were in no danger of invasion, or of being trodden by an hostile army. Distance, intervening forests, rugged roads and large water courses, were obstacles not to be encountered by an enemy, who were dependent on their ships for their supplies, and their safe retreat, in case of reverses.

The freemen of this extensive valley, did not, at this crisis, hold back their movements, either in time, or numbers, for forced requisitions; in retaliation, for the indifference manifested by the citizens of the eastern border of the Province of

---

* Amer. Arch., 5th Ser., 1 Vol., 619. † Ib., 994.

‡ The companies marching from Cumberland county, in August, 1776, were commanded by Captains John Steel, Samuel Postlethwaite, Andrew Galbreath, Samuel McCune, Thomas Turbott, James McConnel, William Huston, Thomas Clark, John Hutton, Robert Culbertson, Charles Lecher, Conrad Schnider, Lieut. Col. Frederick Watts; other Captains were preparing to march. Amer. Arch., 5th Series, 1 Vol., page 619.

Pennsylvania, for sufferings, and privations of the inhabitants of their valley, when, for years, they were exposed to the merciless cruelties of savage enemies, aided and instigated by French power ; though they could not forget, that their repeated supplications to the Provincial government, for measures of defence and protection, during the Indian wars, that were laying waste their settlements, with fire and the blood of women and children, were either disregarded, or met by tardy and inefficient provision, by a government, whose legislation was under the control then, of the representatives of Philadelphia, Chester and Bucks. The brave and hardy men of the Cumberland valley, who had, for ten years, been exercising their strength and vigor to repair the waste and desolation of their homes and property, from which many had been driven ; and for years, compelled to seek for their families, safety in the counties of Lancaster and York, did not allow themselves to think of resentment or retaliation, when the enemy of their country was menacing their State. These patriotic men were too magnanimous and generous, in the hour of danger, and public necessity, to speak, or think of old wrongs, committed against them, by their fellow citizens, or their late government. But a few days were required to arrange their affairs, collect their arms and plain accoutrements, when they marched forth, with drawn swords, and shouldered arms, to meet the public enemy, wherever commanded, either on Pennsylvania soil, on the plains of New Jersey, or elsewhere.

The Presbyterian element, was still not only the predominant, but almost the universal one, in this valley. Its influence, at this juncture, was pervading and powerful in behalf of the liberties and independence of the country. The tendencies of the Presbyterian influence, was to a Republican government, to which, in its organization of ministerial parity and workings, it was most analogous. This was manifested by the early movements of Presbyterian communities in Pennsylvania, Virginia and North Carolina, advocating independence by the American colonies of the British government, and the declaration of that independence. It was also manifested by the prompt, zealous, active, and praiseworthy coöperation of Presbyterians, by their voluntary enrollment to form and maintain, the army of the Revolution and the independence of the colonies.

The company in the lead, in July, 1776, from Carlisle, was that under the command of the Rev. Capt. John Steele, the pastor of the Presbyterian congregation, worshipping in or near Carlisle. We have before noticed Mr. Steele, as pastor of the Presbyterian church on west Conococheague, in the same county, during the Indian wars that followed Braddock's defeat. Having received there, the appointment of Provincial Captain, he officiated as the Captain of a company of rangers, as well as Pastor of a congregation, to whom he preached until they were dispersed by the savages and driven into exile. In these wars he had acquired military training and experience, which were now at the service of his country against the army of his late, but now rejected royal master.

The spirit manifested in this valley, by its many volunteers, had been fostered, by the Presbyterian clergymen of the congregations, throughout its extent. Whilst they addressed the people, as sinners and fallen men, on their duties as Christians, they made eloquent appeals to their feelings, as citizens, in behalf of the liberties and independence of American freemen.

In rousing the spirit of patriotism and resistance, there was no Presbyterian clergyman more active and influential, than the Rev. John King, then pastor on west Conococheague. Many of his addresses and discourses, during the exciting times of the Revolution, were in writing, and are preserved; extended extracts from some of them, are given in the "Churches of the Valley," by the Rev. Alfred Nevin, which are creditable to Dr. King, as a Christian minister and American patriot. His sincerity and zeal were attested by his going with his church-members, as their chaplain, to the seat of war.

Dr. King was born in Lancaster county, at Chesnut Level, in 1740. His father, Robert King, who resided there, was an emigrant from Ireland, and a minister in the Presbyterian Church. Mr. John King commenced his classical studies under Mr. Smith, and also at Newark Academy. He established, about 1760, a classical school in the Cumberland valley, on west Conococheague, which he pursued, to the education of young men, for three years, until the Indian ravages and murders in the settlements disbanded his school. His sister was killed there by the savages. Mr. King, after being compelled to leave the Conococheague settlement, on account of the Indian wars, and the flight of the inhabitants, returned eastward, and after a short time, entered Philadelphia College, then under the care of Drs. William Smith, and Francis Allison. Whilst prosecuting his studies in the College, he, at the same time, taught one of the higher classes in the Academy, which was connected with it. He graduated in 1766, and was licensed to preach in 1767. In 1792, Dickinson College conferred on him the degree of Doctor of Divinity. He had good talents, which were diligently cultivated. Beside being a good Latin and Greek scholar, he had made himself well acquainted with the Hebrew and French. The natural and exact sciences had received a good deal of his attention, whilst he was well acquainted with theology and ecclesiastical history. His reputation for ability and learning, with an extensive library, attracted to him young men, whom he received into his family, for the prosecution of their theological studies, preparatory to the ministry. Amongst these were the Rev. David Elliott, D. D., of Allegheny Seminary, and the late Rev. Matthew Brown, D. D., President of Jefferson College. Dr. King continued in his pastoral charge, from 1769 till 1811, when he resigned, on account of health and bodily infirmity, having been eminently useful and much beloved and respected.

No less zealous, in the cause of Independence, was the Rev. John Craighead, pastor of the Presbyterian congregation at Rocky Spring, near Chambersburg, where he had been ordained in 1768. "Though he did not fail to preach Jesus Christ, the only hope of salvation, it is said, after the delivery of this sacred message to fallen and sinful men, on one occasion, he exhorted, in eloquent and patriotic strains, the youth of the congregation, to rise up and join the noble band then engaged under Washington, in struggling to free our beloved country from British oppression. It is related that, upon another occasion, this patriotic preacher declaimed, from the pulpit, in such burning and powerful terms, against the wrongs they were then suffering, that after one glowing description of the duty of the men, the whole congregation rose from their seats and declared their willingness to march to the conflict."* The members of his congregation did most heroically march, in July, 1776, and joined the American army under the command of Washington, in New Jersey, and which he accompanied as chaplain; and with that company, was made prisoner, at Long Island, or Fort Washington. He remained the pastor of this congregation until 1799, the year of his death ; "having, by his fervent and eloquent ministry, been instrumental, under Providence, in winning many souls, from darkness and sin to light and life, through a merciful Redeemer."

The estimate put on patriotism, associated with religious character, by the Presbyterian Church, in the Revolutionary times, is attested in the life of the Rev. James Crawford, who, when a student, had been obliged to leave Princeton College, without his Degree, owing to the interruption of the College exercises, by the British army, and being inclined to emigrate south, he carried with him, from his pastor, the Rev. John Craighead, whom, we suppose to have been the ardent whig of that name, referred to in 1777, a certificate of his church-membership, and who appended to it a representation, deemed essential to his credit, and to the hospitality, fellowship and friendship of the Presbyterian settlements, where this student of divinity might visit, and where he might be disposed to take up his abode. That addition, to the usual certificate, was in these words: "and also, he appears well affected to the cause of American liberty."†

The Rev. Robert Cooper, D. D., pastor of the Presbyterian congregation at Middle Spring, near Shippensburg, was also an ardent whig, who encouraged the members of his congregation to join with arms, the standard of their country. His congregation shared his spirit and resolution, and were part of

---

* Churches of the Valley, 185. † Davidson's His. Ch. of Ky., 80.

the force of volunteers that marched from Carlisle in August, 1776, accompanied by their brave, patriotic and pious minister. He returned to his pastoral charge, where he continued to minister acceptably and usefully until 1797, when he resigned. "Dr. Cooper was esteemed a man of sound and strong mind, as well as a divine of great judiciousness and piety." He was one of the Committee appointed in 1785, by the Synods of Philadelphia and New York, to revise the standards of the Church, which led to the adoption and establishment of the present plan.

That a like patriotic spirit pervaded the Scotch Irish race, of this Presbyterian community, is evinced by the number of military companies, sixteen, that volunteered in July, 1776, to sustain, by their persons and lives, the Independence that was proclaimed. One of these companies from the neighborhood of Chambersburg, was made up of men of Irish and German nativity, and was commanded by Captain Conrad Schnider, of the German Reformed Church, having for his first Lieutenant, John Crawford, of Irish nativity and Presbyterian connection.

This valley, with the small adjacent ones, known as Path and Sherman's valleys, continued, throughout the Revolutionary struggle, to furnish, from time to time, reinforcements of men for the army, as the public exigencies required. In the Cumberland valley, almost every man able to carry arms and endure a soldier's life, had been in the military service of his country. Some performed more than one tour of service, whilst others remained in the army, under every exposure, trial, good and bad fortune, from the beginning of the war till the end of it, when Independence was acknowledged and peace proclaimed.

These ready volunteers were farmers of substance, intelligence, and respectability ; many of them the heads of families, who were left behind. Some of the officers, as well as the men in the ranks, were ruling elders in the Presbyterian congregations with which they worshipped. Throughout this great valley, a Tory, a name applied, in Revolutionary times, to a person opposed to the war, and in favor of British claims, was rare, if to be found at all. Not to be zealous in the cause of American Independence, was a reproach, that not only subjected the suspected individual to public disfavor, but in some instances, brought down upon him, the notice or discipline of the church. The writer of this, saw, many years since, amongst the papers of a deceased elder of the Presbyterian Church of Chambersburg, an ancient writing, purporting to be a charge preferred to the session of that church, against one of its members, that "*he is strongly suspected of not being sincere in his professions of attachment to the cause of the Revolution.*" What action was had on this accusation, by the church court, did not appear, and the minutes of the church of that period, were not preserved by the church officers. It is supposed, that the member accused, exculpated himself from a charge, which, in that community, was not only disreputable, but degrading. This suspected person, was well known to the writer, as a farmer in the neighborhood, who lived in good circumstances on his farm till his death, about 1800, respected as a good and orderly citizen, leaving descendants of influence and distinction.

In the notice by the Supreme Executive Council of Pennsylvania, of April 12th 1779,* for the sale of the forfeited estates of persons attainted of Treason, embracing the names of numbers in Philadelphia, and some in several of the neighboring counties, there was not one in the county of Cumberland. Amongst those at that time proclaimed as *traitors*, were Joseph Galloway and Andrew Allen, Esqs. Galloway had been Speaker of the Assembly of Pennsylvania, and both had been members of the Congress of 1776, and opposed the Declaration of Independence. And also Jacob Duche, an Episcopal minister, of Philadelphia, who, on the nomination of Samuel Adams, a stiff Congregationalist, had been appointed *chaplain* to the first Continental Congress. When the British General, Howe, entered Philadelphia, 1778, "Duche was among the traitors that welcomed him into the possession of the Capitol of the State, and had the effrontery of writing and sending a letter to Washington, advising him to give over the ungodly cause in which he was engaged.†"

* Col. Rec. Vol. 9, p. 745. † Hild. His., 3, p. 221,

The eminent John Dickinson, who opposed in Congress, the Declaration of Independence, as *premature;* yet, when it was adopted, and the public resentment had prostrated him, he had still a patriotism in his heart, that would neither allow him to go over with his colleagues, Galloway and Allen, to the enemy, or to remain neutral, but at the head of a regiment of which he was Colonel, he repaired at once to the aid of his country, as a part of the flying camp in New Jersey.

The Cumberland valley furnished to military service, in the Revolutionary army, from its inhabitants, officers General Armstrong and Irwin, Colonels Magaw, Chambers, Watts, Blair, Smith, Wilson, Montgomery, Buchanan, and others, and Majors, Captains and subalterns, in numbers too great to be enumerated here; whilst its soldiers, in the rank and file, were in number, little below the taxables of their district.

The Scotch Irish settlers, with their immediate descendants, from the counties of Lancaster and York, in Pennsylvania, gave up to their country, in the Revolutionary conflict, their brave, vigorous, and patriotic men, who, in the camp and battle field, were shoulder to shoulder with their Cumberland fellow soldiers, to do and serve, as they were commanded.

Officers and men, of this race, from the counties named, accompanied Arnold in the campaign for the invasion of Canada in 1775, which they prosecuted amid hardships, privations, toils and sufferings indescribable, through a trackless wilderness of several hundred miles ; and joined in the storming of Quebec, in which they were repulsed, by an overwhelming British force, under which, the brave and gallant General Montgomery, of Irish nativity, fell, mortally wounded, and many were made prisoners.

Other volunteers, of the same race, from the same counties, overpowered by the superior force of the enemy at Fort Washington, were there made prisoners, and endured for years, in and near New York, a captivity, that was oppressive and cruel to officers and privates, under which many were made victims.

Others, of like national origin, from the same places, were with the army, under Washington, when it crossed the Delaware, with its floating ice, in mid-winter, and darkness, in the vicinity of their exulting and powerful enemy, and marched on the frozen earth, with bare and bleeding feet, to gain his rear, and surprised him by the capture of his Hessian mercenaries, when he was reposing in the security, that the army of Washington had fled and was dispersed.

Others, from the same Scotch Irish settlements, were in that desperate assault, under General Wayne, at Stony Point, an almost inaccessible height, defended by a garrison of six hundred men, and a strong battery of artillery, which were attacked at midnight, by brave American freemen, with unloaded muskets and fixed bayonets, and who carried it without firing a single gun—taking five hundred and forty-three prisoners—being one of the most brilliant exploits of the war.

The same men were also, in numbers, in the battles of Brandywine, Germantown and Monmouth. There were, on a few occasions, trepidations and insubordination, amongst some portion of the Pennsylvania militia, when, without discipline or experience, they were brought suddenly to encounter the well trained, and well equipped forces of the enemy, that had been long inured to service, and the conflict of arms.

General Armstrong, in a communication to the State Executive, Dec., 1777,* whilst he complains of the conduct of some of the militia, of his State, says: "They judge ill of the uses of a body of men, who fix their character from a single action, and still worse, who brand the whole with the infamous conduct of only a part, when others, of the same body, and on the same occasion, have fully evinced their bravery. Taken as a body, the militia have rendered that service, that neither the State nor the army, could have dispensed with. They have met and skirmished with the enemy, as early and as often as others, and, except the battle of Brandywine, of which, from their station, little fell in their way, *have had a proportional share of success, hazard and loss of blood.*"

It was not only a hard military service, in which the Scotch Irish of Pennsylvania, were efficient, and distinguished, during the Revolutionary war, but their men were of eminence and

---

* Penn. Arch., Vol. 6, p. 100.

influence, in the Councils of the National, as well as of the State government, during these times, that called forth the talents, energies, abilities, bravery and patriotism of the country. McKean, of Philadelphia, Wilson, of Cumberland, and Smith of York, could, as Colonels, be at the head of their regiments in the army, often to inspire and lead their men, as well as to expose themselves in their command against the enemy, and also serve as the Representatives of their constituents in Congress. Their services in Congress were neither few nor small, and though without the peril of life and blood of the battle field, they were arduous, and of great responsibility. They were all working members, and as members of various committees, had committed to them the most important duties and trusts, for the public welfare, which were executed by them with a wisdom, intelligence, and judgment, that commended them to the Congress and the country. In November, 1776, Mr. Wilson and Mr. Smith, were both appointed, with Messrs. Chase, Clymer and Stockton, by Congress, an Executive Committee, who were charged with full powers to carry on the *whole business of the war;* "to devise and execute measures for effectually reinforcing General Washington, and obstructing the progress of General Howe's army." This measure showed the unbounded confidence of Congress in the wisdom judgment, virtue and firmness of the Committee, for a delegation to them of the powers of Congress. Col. Smith, with part of the committee, visited the army and General Washington, and were "so impressed with the insuperable difficulties of their task, the importance of the crisis, and the abilities of the Commander in Chief, with whom alone, they were convinced, such powers could be advantageously placed."

Col. McKean was the commander of a Regiment, a Delegate to Congress from Delaware, the President of Congress, and Chief Justice of the State of Pennsylvania, combining, at one time, all these offices. The papers emanating from the Congress of the Colonies and of the States, were distinguished for style, ability, moderation and firmness, as well as unexampled elevation and dignity of sentiment; and evinced the talents and high character of the members of the body, as scholars and statesmen. It was a high eulogium of the Congress of 1775, when Lord Chatham declared, "that though he had studied and admired the free States of antiquity, the master spirits of the world, yet, for solidity of reasoning, force of sagacity and wisdom of conclusion, no body of men could stand in preference to this Congress."

History records no instance of a political body, charged with more important public duties, and responsibilities, than the Congress of the American colonies. It had to organize in the midst of war and revolution, a new and untried government, for the union of thirteen separate colonies. It had to provide for the military and civil establishments of that government; conduct war against one of the oldest and most powerful governments of the Old World; regulate commerce; create and collect revenue. It had to legislate, not only against the public enemy, but also against tories and traitors, within their fold. The men who discharged these trusts with wisdom, integrity, labor and devotion to their country, were men of no common energy, ability and purity. Our country was one of destiny for great purposes. Amongst the eminent public men of Pennsylvania, during the Revolutionary war, as well as in the years preceding, of controversy with the mother country, in relation to Colonial rights, illegal taxation, and Parliamentary usurpation, there was no one more distinguished for his civil and military services, and many virtues, than Joseph Reed, of the city of Philadelphia, whose active life, was one of untiring devotion to the best interests of Pennsylvania and the nation; enjoying the public confidence and regard for ability, integrity and patriotism, to a degree only surpassed by the Father of his country. He was the military secretary of Washington at Cambridge—Adjutant General of the Continental army—member of the Congress of the United States, and President of the Executive Council of the State of Pennsylvania.* Whilst a kind Providence raised up for the

* President Reed, was of Irish descent, and had selected Philadelphia as his residence in the profession of the Law, with all the advantages of education afforded by the best Institutions in the Colonies, and by an attendance at the Inns of Court for two years. His life and correspondence, edited by his grandson, the Hon. William B. Reed, is one of the most valuable, and in-

Colonies a Washington, to direct and command their army, we may believe, that the same Providential care formed for the times, the eminent and virtuous men, who composed its early Congress.

The Scotch Irish element in the several counties of Pennsylvania, had, during the Revolution, its full representation in the Executive Council of the State and Assembly, and in having at the head of its Judiciary, Chief Justice McKean.

In those days, requiring clear heads, honest hearts, and sage statesmen, we do not find any historical record of elevated character, reproaching the Scotch Irish with being a "hot-headed race, excitable in temper, unrestrainable in passion, invincible in prejudice." They occupied, with public approbation and respect, the high places in the judiciary, the floor of Congress, in the committee room, and in the executive government.

The emigration of the Scotch Irish from Pennsylvania, before the Revolution, was southward, into Virginia and N. Carolina. The first public road in the Kittochtinny valley, west of the Susquehanna, was laid out in 1735, by order of the Court of Lancaster, from Harris' Ferry, on the Susquehanna, to the Potomac river at Williams' Ferry, in the same valley. The travel and emigration was in that direction, for several reasons. The country was more accessible, than over the mountains, by the Traders' or Indians' paths .The country in Pennsylvania, west of the Allegheny mountain, was not open to settlement and purchase, until 1769, the cession from the Indians being obtained by the Proprietaries the preceding year. Settlements had been made in North Carolina, by Irish and Scotch emigrants, as early as 1730, who had landed at Charleston, South Carolina, and some in Virginia, about the same time. The Kittochtinny valley, south of the Potomac, was attractive to settlers, as well as what was north of that river. The settle-

---

teresting contributions to our Revolutionary History, and more particularly to the participation of Pennsylvania and its citizens, in that memorable struggle. It is illustrated and verified by the various correspondence of Washington, and others, prominent actors in the *times that tried men's souls.* At the early age of forty-four, his active and useful life was closed by disease, in a constitution worn out in the service of his country.

ments in that portion of this valley, between the Susquehanna and Potomac rivers, were, as before stated, retarded to a considerable extent, until 1737, as the purchase of it, by the Proprietary of Pennsylvania, from the Indians, was only effected in 1736, after which, the Land office was opened for the sale of lands, in the established manner, and the controversy in relation to the Maryland boundary, was quieted by the Royal order, the same year.

The greater security in North Carolina, from Indian hostilities, induced some of the Pennsylvania Scotch Irish settlers, to emigrate to the neighborhood of friends, or relatives, resident in that southern State. Amongst those emigrating from the Kittochtinny valley, west of the Susquehanna, which had not then received the name of the Cumberland valley, was the father of the Rev. James Hall, D. D., of Treadwell county, North Carolina. Dr. Hall was of Scotch Irish parentage, and born in that valley in 1744, near where Carlisle was afterwards located. In eight years after, his father removed with his family, to North Carolina. Dr. Hall, who graduated at Nassau Hall, Princeton, in 1774, became an eminent Presbyterian minister, and patriot, distinguished for talents, attainments, and usefulness. He gave his powers of mind, body and estate to the cause of his country. He not only officiated as chaplain in the army, but organized and commanded a military company for some time, in the Revolutionary war. To enable young men to acquire a knowledge of the sciences, who could not afford the expense of attending a northern college, he, like the elder Tennent, in Pennsylvania, established at his own house, "an Academy of the Sciences," being himself the sole proprietor, and for which he purchased a philosophical apparatus. A large number of eminent men received their scientific education there, besides a number of ministers who studied theology under his direction. His character for talents, and piety, and public spirit, his soundness as a theologian, his great facility in imparting instruction, and his well selected library, caused his *house* to become a school of the prophets, from which came out some of the best ministers of southern Zion.*

After the acknowledgement of National Independence, and permanent relations of peace, being established with foreign countries, as well as with the Indian tribes, the inhabitants of Cumberland county resumed their industrial occupations in the cultivation of their farms, and the few who were mechanics, in their respective employments. The taste for rural life, was still the prevailing one, and the occupation preferred, was that of agriculture. In this entire valley, from the Susquehanna to the Maryland line, there were, after the close of the Revolutionary war, but three villages, viz: Carlisle, Shippensburg, and Chambersburg, containing severally, but a few hundred inhabitants. Franklin county, separated from Cumberland county in 1784, had, within its entire boundary, but one town, Chambersburg, the place of holding the Courts and county Offices.

The inhabitants of Cumberland county, immediately after the Revolutionary war, showing their appreciation of a high grade for the education of young men in science, literature, and theology, turned their attention to the establishment of a College, within their bounds. They did not wait to repair the losses and sacrifices, to which they had subjected themselves, by a military service, in distant places, during the protracted war for American Independence, before they would provide for elevated education. They were ready to act at once in the matter, and this at a time when the governments of the State, as well as the Confederation, were embarrassed with war debts, want of financial resources, and a confederation of independent States, that was deficient in effective provisions, and in strength, was little better than a rope of sand. The people were also called on to meet heavy taxation for local, State and National purposes, with little or no currency of value, and with very limited resources. Yet, the spirit that animated with energy and resolution, the men who had encountered the wilderness, defended the frontiers of the colony, against the savages and

* Foote's Sketches of North Carolina, 330.

their French allies, and given themselves up to the defence of their country, against royal despotism and parliamentary usurpation, induced them to give their energies and perseverance, recruited by a short period of peace, to provide for education, by an institution that would be worthy of public confidence and respect. Measures were taken to collect funds for it, and in 1783, a charter was obtained from the Legislature, by which the Institution was located at Carlisle, and called Dickinson College, in commemoration of John Dickinson, President of the Supreme Executive Council of the State, who had been liberal in his donation to it. The first faculty organized in 1784, consisted of the Rev. Charles Nesbit, of Montrose, Scotland, as President; James Ross, Professor of Languages, to which was added, the year following, Rev. Robert Davidson, D. D., Professor of Belles Lettres, and Robert Johnston, Instructor of Mathematics. Under the auspices of this Faculty and Instructors, who were eminently qualified by abilities and learning, and who adopted a high standard of education for their graduates, the College prospered, and acquired a high reputation, that attracted to it many students, not only from Pennsylvania, but from other States. During the Presidency of Dr. Nesbit, there graduated many young men of celebrity, as lawyers, jurists and statesmen, in this and other States, and from the teachings of this College and the theological lectures of Dr. Nesbit to classes, preparatory to the ministry, there were given to the Presbyterian Church, a number of ministers of distinction for talents, acquirements, piety and usefulness.

This Institution sustained a severe loss, in the death of Dr. Nesbit, in 1804. Dr. Davidson, Professor, and Pastor of the Presbyterian church in Carlisle, was his successor for four years, as President *pro tem.*, when Dr. Atwater was appointed President.

This Institution was founded, in a great measure, by the Scotch Irish Presbyterians of Cumberland, and neighboring counties in Pennsylvania, who, with the ministers of that Church, continued to foster and patronize it for many years, during which, it was successful, and very useful, in giving to the country, many well educated men. It had not been endowed sufficiently, to sustain a faculty, with the high qualifications desired and demanded. Dr. Atwater, and a succession of other Presidents, resigned, after short terms, which was prejudicial to the interests of the Institution, as no one retained the Presidency long enough, after Dr. Nesbit, to give it a decided reputation.

Its first faculty were of Scotch nativity, or Irish descent, and Presbyterian in their religious creed, associations and worship. This predominance of Presbyterianism, in the Principals and Professors, was continued, with a few exceptions, for a series of years. The majority of its Trustees belonged to the same denomination. Though the pervading character of this Institution was Presbyterian, yet, it was not sectarian in its ruling influence. There was no influence exercised to make proselytes amongst its students, from the ranks of other denominations, and the Institution had the respect and confidence of the public, as long as there were abilities, learning and attention in its faculty, and efficiency in its government. The interest of many, who had favored it, abated, and efforts to sustain it, even by the Presbyterian Church, were relaxed, and for a number of years it continued to languish, with occasional temporary revivals, and spasmodic efforts to regain, under a new President, some of its former vigor and reputation. This was, in a great measure, attributed to the want of attention and interest, on the part of its Trustees, and to dissensions prevailing with that portion of them living in the vicinity, to whom, as is usual, with literary and religious Institutions, its management was chiefly committed. The Trustees of Carlisle and its neighborhood, constituted its business board, for the management of most of the concerns of the College; and either discouraged, by failures of measures adopted to sustain the College, or from unhappy dissensions amongst themselves, dividing them, chose to give away the Institution, with all its property, and corporate privileges ; and then abandon their trust, by resignation, to make their donation effective. There can be no reflection on our Methodist brethren, in being parties to the negotiation. This large donation was cast into their lap. They could not well decline it, when all the advantages were on their side. Their success was complete, and the Methodist Episcopal Church obtained the control of Dickinson College in 1833, which they have exercised ever since. They have treated it as an Institution of their Church, by awakening an interest with their denomination, to endeavor to endow and sustain it. The zeal, abilities, and perseverance of its Trustees and Faculty, immediately imparted to it the vigor which it wanted, and made it extensively useful in diffusing education.

What was the gain of the Methodist Episcopal Church, was the loss of the Presbyterian, whose members and ministers, had been the founders and patrons of this Institution, and who had given their money, as well as their time, labor and services, to its establishment and organization.*

The Synod of Philadelphia, within whose bounds this College was, had not the vigilance, activity, and zeal, for the preservation of its Institutions, in which men were to be educated for the ministry, that characterized that Synod in its early history, or it would not have closed its eyes to the usefulness of this Institution to the Church and State, slumbered over its decline, or have allowed it, with all its property, advantages, and privileges to be given away to any other religious denomination, however respectable.

It becomes this ecclesiastical body, and the Baltimore Synod, to make a vigorous effort to recover their lost ground, retrieve their supineness, and supply, for Presbyterian education and influence, an Institution in middle Pennsylvania, wherein young men may receive a preparatory education, that may qualify them for the ministry, or learned professions, which induced the establishment, in early times, when the country was new, of the Log and other Colleges, by Presbyterian ministers, and the members of the Presbyterian Church.

* The writer acknowledges himself as one of the remote and delinquent Trustees referred to, and though not one of the board that made the transfer, to which measure he had made known his opposition, and in execution of it, he did not resign; yet, he does not exculpate himself on account of absence, as it was his duty to have been present, and oppose the measure, with what influence he might possess, if advised of the intended action, and was able to attend.

There are amongst the descendants of the Scotch Irish settlers, at this time, within the bounds of these Synods, four fold the means and resources, which their ancestors had, when they established colleges, which have contributed much to elevate and extend education. The number of Presbyterian churches in the Cumberland valley, including Path valley, when Dickinson College was established, were sixteen; the number at this time, within the same bounds, is over thirty. Though the Presbyterian worshippers, have, in some of the rural congregations, in the Cumberland valley, diminished, by reason of the removal of the members west, or to other residences, yet this has been much more than supplied, by new and additional Presbyterian churches, in the towns and villages of the same valley. Such an Institution, established west of the Susquehanna, in middle Pennsylvania, would be incalculably useful, without interfering with, or prejudicing kindred Institutions, of like character, on the eastern or western borders of our great State.

CHAPTER V.

Instrumentality of the Scotch Irish schools and seminaries in Pennsylvania in the education of young men for usefulness in other Colonies—In Virginia: Robinson, Davies, Waddell, the Messrs. Smiths—In North Carolina: McAden, Caldwell—New Jersey: Establishment of Nassau Hall, Princeton—Maryland: Baltimore church organization—F. Allison.

It is difficult to measure, or estimate the advantages to society and the country, from the establishment of the academies and schools of the Tennents, Blairs, Finley, Smith, and Allison, in eastern Pensylvania, during the early part of the eighteenth century. Many young men were enabled to obtain within those schools, an education on terms, and in a manner not to be procured any where else in the middle colonies; and who, without such facilities, must have been withheld from the intellectual education they desired, and which was necessary to elevate them to stations of distinction and public usefulness.

Young men of good and studious habits, with abilities of an high order and respectability, sought these seminaries, and in the plain buildings appropriated to education, under the teaching and direction of these eminent and faithful instructors, acquired an amount of knowledge, that deservedly gave them the reputation of scholars, in classical literature, and mathematical proficiency; whilst those, pursuing their theological studies, preparatory to the ministry, testified, by their attainments, success and eminent usefulness, that their labors had been well directed, and improved, not only to their advantage as candidates, but to that of extending religious influence, as well as moral and intellectual education.

From the Log College of the Tennents, first emanated men, some of whom, were to be shining lights of the age, in the Gospel ministry, and who devoted their talents and attainments, in proclaiming the unsearchable riches of Christ. Others, combined with the ministry, the office of teacher, in Seminaries established, in other localities, after the model of the original Log College.

The influence of these seminaries, established, conducted, and maintained in the early history of the Province, by the Scotch Irish Presbyterian ministers, was of inestimable usefulness to the inhabitants of Pennsylvania. They gave to the rapidly increasing communities, made up of Irish and Scotch emigrants, an educated, zealous and pious ministry, sound in the faith, and a church organization by Presbyters, that was to the desire and acceptance of the great mass of the people. In the same schools, the young men of Pennsylvania, and of some other colonies, received a classical and scientific education, that prepared some for high places in the medical profession, whilst others were educated there, preparatory to the study of the law, and acquired, deservedly, the reputation and places of jurists, lawyers and statesmen.

From these fountains of education, issued streams of knowledge that flowed beyond the bounds of Pennsylvania, into other colonies. Young men of talents, learning and piety, from these schools, were the instruments, in the hands of Divine Providence, of carrying to the destitute districts of neighboring and distant colonies, the means and facilities of improved education, and a pious and evangelical ministry. Amongst these instruments of early missionary labor, was the Rev. Wm. Robinson, who was sent as an evangelist, by the Presbytery of New Castle, in the winter of 1742–3, in consequence of the earnest solicitations of the people, to visit the Presbyterian settlements in the valley of the Shenandoah, and some parts of Virginia, then destitute of a ministry. He entered on his mission with zeal and perseverance, and though incommoded and obstructed on entering Virginia by intolerance, and arrest, for preaching without a license from the Governor, he was permitted to proceed to North Carolina; and on his return, preached in Hanover county, Virginia, the first sermon heard there from a Presbyterian minister. He continued preaching four days, successively, to large and increasing audiences, with a power, and success, in awaking the careless, instructing the ignorant, that was wonderful and unprecedented, and with impressions that were lasting and permanent, and to the conversion of many. His engagements, elsewhere, to visit the destitute districts in Virginia, soliciting the preaching of the Gospel, by a minister of sound and practical piety, took him from Hanover. The audiences that had heard his discourses there, with so much interest and profit, proposed to renumerate him for his services, which he declined. The money raised, was, without his knowledge, put into his saddle-bags, by the gentleman at whose house he lodged. When he afterwards discovered it, he refused to appropriate it to his own use, though his means were small, and applied it to aid Samuel Davies, then a student at Fagg's Manor, Pennsylvania, pursuing his studies under the care of the Rev. Samuel Blair, for the ministry. By an inscrutable Providence, whose ways are those of infinite wisdom, and past the finding out of short-sighted men, Mr. Robinson, this eminent and faithful steward of his Lord and Master, was removed from his labors on earth, in April, 1746. He was a martyr, it was believed, to the labors he voluntarily endured for the cause of Christ, in Virginia and North Carolina. He bequeathed his library to his young friend, protege and fellow-laborer, the Rev. Samuel Davies, on whom his mantle may be supposed to have fallen.*

Next in order of time, we may name the Rev. Samuel Davies, alluded to. He was of Welsh descent, and born in New Castle county, Delaware, then Pennsylvania. Having been licensed by the Presbytery of New Castle, in 1745, he visited Virginia, and located himself permanently there in 1748, in the county of Hanover, where his friend, the Rev. Mr. Robinson, had, as a pioneer, assisted in opening the way for Gospel instruction and ordinances, some years before. Mr. Davies, in eloquence, piety, and learning, had no superior, was called "the prince of preachers," and acquired a greater influence, than any other preacher in Virginia ever possessed. From this field of labor and usefulness, Mr. Davies was withdrawn, by his election to the Presidency of the College of New Jersey, in 1759, where he continued until his death in 1761, at the age of thirty-seven.

James Waddell, distinguished in Virginia history and literature as a scholar and orator, eminent for eloquence and piety, was brought, in 1739, from Ireland, an infant in the arms of his mother, to Pennsylvania, selected by his parents as their place of abode. Having been disabled in the use of his hand, by an accidental blow from an axe in the hand of a brother, his parents, in consequence of this disability, were induced to seek for him a liberal education, for which, his powers of mind were admirably adapted. His progress at the "Log College" of Dr. Finley, at Nottingham, was rapid. His attainments in the Greek and Latin studies, were of so high an order, as to occasion his promotion, when a youth, to the office of Tutor, in the Nottingham academy, as well as in that of Rev. Robert Smith, of Pequea, of Lancaster county. Having acquired great proficiency in his studies, at the age of nineteen he removed from Pennsylvania southward, and on his way, formed the acquaintance of the Rev. Samuel Davies, in Virginia, where he was induced to remain, taking charge of a classical

* Foote's Sketches of Virginia.

school of Louisa, and commenced the studies, preparatory for the sacred ministry in Virginia, which, thenceforth, became his home. In 1761, he was licensed by the Presbytery, and in the same year, several calls were put into his hands from vacant churches in Virginia, and also one from the neighborhood of York, Pennsylvania, and of the many promising fields of labor, as a minister, presented to him, he made choice of the lower part of the great northern neck in Virginia, between the rivers Potomac and Rappahannoc. His interesting, useful, and successful labors, as a minister, in the northern neck, were ended in the early part of the Revolutionary war, by his removal to the valley of Shenandoah in 1778, occasioned by the emigration of leading persons in his congregations, to the mountainous regions, and his impaired health, from bilious attacks, in the northern neck. The call of General Green, for aid to resist Cornwallis, in his invasion, was responded to promptly by the Scotch Irish members of Mr. Waddell's pastoral charge, who, before their departure for the camp, met them in arms, and preached to them a pastor's farewell, which, to many, were the last words they ever heard from the lips of their revered pastor.

Mr. Waddell's great affliction, was an incurable blindness. Though blind, he was devoted to books ; his wife and children spending hours daily in reading to him. Owing to this, his powers of mind were not impaired by his loss of sight, and he retained his usual flow of spirits, which often arose to hilarity. He never declaimed in the pulpit, but prepared his exercises for that place with study.

The graphic description, by the eminent and eloquent Wirt, of Waddell, the blind preacher, is indelibly impressed on the pages of Virginia history. It has been compared to the poems of Homer, which immortalized the writer as well as his hero. Mr. Waddell died in 1805, with great Christian serenity, universally beloved, and his body was carried to the grave by his servants, who performed this last service with reverence and grief.

Virginia was also indebted to the same schools, for the distinguished and learned Rev. Samuel Stanhope Smith, and Rev.

John Blair Smith, D. D., brothers of Irish descent, born and educated at the Log academy, of their father, Robert Smith, D. D., in the county of Lancaster, Pennsylvania, and graduates of the College of New Jersey, at Princeton. The Rev. S. S. Smith, having been licensed by the New Castle Presbytery, visited, in 1771, Virginia, as a missionary, when he at once saw the necessity of a literary institution in Virginia, and aided and encouraged the efforts of Hanover Presbytery to call it into being. He became the projector and founder of Hampden Sidney College in that colony. Notwithstanding the exciting times of the Revolution, in 1775, Mr. Smith, with the aid of this Presbytery, proceeded to collect funds for the establishment of the projected literary institution. "The Presbytery, it is stated, proceeded to take steps to have Mr. Smith settled as a preacher as well as a teacher, according to the spirit of the '*Log College*,' in Pennsylvania, which had been so rich in blessings on Virginia." Mr. Smith was chosen Rector of the infant institution, then called the academy of Prince Edward, and shortly after of Hampden Sidney College, and also installed pastor of the united congregations of Cumberland and Prince Edward. Amongst the Trustees selected for this humble institution of Presbyterian origin, and Scotch Irish affinities, were James Madison, Jr., afterwards Chief Magistrate of the United States, and Patrick Henry, the distinguished orator, and Governor of Virginia.

The College was organized by the appointment of Mr. John B. Smith, brother of the principal, as first assistant, and Mr. Samuel Doak, as second assistant. From the increase of students, beyond expectation, Mr. David Witherspoon was appointed third assistant. Hampden Sidney went on prosperously, increasing in reputation and usefulness, having one hundred and ten students the first summer, notwithstanding the Revolutionary contest.

The terms of this academy, when opened in 1776, were £8 for board; and for washing and bed, £3 per year. So great was the desire of the youth of the Scotch Irish race of Virginia to avail themselves of the advantages to be enjoyed in education, under the teachings of the Messrs. Smith, at their log college, that there was a scarcity of apartments for their accommodation, and whilst the new academy building was in rapid progress, many of the students erected small temporary huts, with the shingles prepared for the academy. In these they were packed close, and with a plank for three or four boys to sit upon, where they diligently pursued their studies till a late hour of the night. From the difficulty of obtaining board and lodging for the numbers that thronged for admission, Messrs. N. Venable and P. Carrington, public men of eminence, honored for their patriotism and religion, built houses for their sons to occupy.

The Messrs. Smith from Pennsylvania, with the aid of the friends of liberty, and religious and moral education in Virginia, in Revolutionary times, surmounted obstacles that would now be deemed appalling, and excited an enthusiasm seldom equalled, to establish in that State a Seminary of learning, for the higher branches of education, after the model of the unpretending, but useful log colleges of Pennsylvania.

In 1779, the Rev. Samuel S. Smith, having had an invitation from the Trustees of New Jersey College, to accept the office of Professor of Moral Philosophy in that Institution, with the approbation of the Presbytery, accepted, and shortly after was made president of the same Institution. His brother, the Rev. John Blair Smith, was appointed his successor of Hampden Sidney, under whose Presidency, this College, on the model of the Log College of Pennsylvania, prospered, both in its theological and literary department, in a manner never surpassed in succeeding years. The President having also accepted the call of the churches of Cumberland and Briery, united the offices of Pastor with the Presidency of College and the Professor of Theology, embracing work for three men, and giving a Christian spirit to the efforts for the education of youth. With him, men of the greatest probity and of the highest public estimation and private worth, were associated in the direction of this Seminary, " where the purest sentiments of religion and patriotism, were inculcated in a most efficient manner."

" President Smith's preaching," says Dr. Hill, " was of the

most animating, pungent, practical character, feeling close for the conscience, and applying truth home to the heart."

Dr. Hoge, who was President of the same College, in speaking of Dr. J. B. Smith, said: " A preacher possessing every ministerial qualification, in a degree so eminent, I have never known; nor do I ever expect again to hear a preacher, whose discourses will be equally calculated for the learned and unlearned, the rich and the poor, the devout Christian, and the abandoned profligate; in a word, every character and description of men. Methinks I still see him stand the accredited ambassador of the great King of kings, and Lord of lords, while every feature and every muscle of his face, every word and action, as well as the lightning of his eyes, seem to bespeak a soul on fire."*

The Declaration of American Independence, by the Congress of the Colonies, in 1776, animated the citizens, young and old, of Virginia, as it did their kinsmen in Pennsylvania, and many offered themselves, as soldiers, to redeem the pledge " of *their fortunes and sacred honor*," in the maintenance of that Independence. "Engaged, as the students were, in Hampden Sidney College, in the pursuit of their studies, their hearts were warm on the side of American liberty, and with the arts and sciences, they exercised in military training, and in the rudiments of war. The Rev. John Blair Smith, the first assistant of this Institution, and afterwards its President, was chosen Captain of a company of students, about sixty-five in number, over seventeen years of age. Mr. D. Witherspoon, second assistant, their Lieutenant, and Mr. S. Venable, their Ensign. The students were uniformed, viz: a hunting shirt, died purple, and every student, although under sixteen years of age, was mustered every month."

In 1777, there was a requisition from the Governor, for a company of militia from Prince Edward county, to oppose an expected invasion from the British. All the students of this College, above sixteen years of age, with the advice of their President, the Rev. Samuel Stanhope Smith, exchanged their

* Dr. Foote's Sketches of Virginia.

numbers for No. 1, with the militia of the county, and marched to Williamsburg, under their officers, to obey the Governor's orders.

After the battle of the Cowpens, in 1781, the excitement in the southern country was great, when Morgan and Green were retreating before the superior army of Cornwallis, Captain Morton, having, in two days, raised a company of his neighbors, to join Green. The Rev. John Blair Smith, then President of Hampden Sidney College, set out at once to join the company of Captain Morton, which he overtook in Halifax. The Captain earnestly entreated him to return to Prince Edward, that he could serve the cause more at home, by his exciting patriotic speeches, than by his presence in camp. Worn out by fatigue, the President returned to the College. "Peter Johnson, about sixteen years of age, the son of the donor of the land on which the College was built, offered himself, and was rejected as under age and under size. He nevertheless procured a horse, and offered himself to Lee, and was, with some hesitation, received. He served during that momentous campaign, with great honor, taking a part in several actions, beside the decisive one of Guilford Court House. He was, in after life, a Judge of eminence in his native State."*

The College suffered from the calamities of a protracted war, which, with its desolation, and alarms, was carried into its very neighborhood, and students, in defence of the liberties of their country, gave up their books for war implements, and from their school rooms repaired to the ranks of the Revolutionary army. "When the war was over, the College was in a depressed state. The enthusiasm for education was somewhat abated among the people at large, objects of ambition and speculation, and the repair of broken fortunes and ruined estates, engrossed the great body of the people. There were still patriots, to appreciate the immeasurable importance of the universal dissemination of knowledge, pure morality, and religion, for the preservation of the political liberty and its advantages, acquired by the arms of freemen." The friends of

* Dr. Foote's Sketches of Virginia, 403.

Hampden Sidney, after the war, applied for, and obtained, from the Legislature, in 1783, a charter for the Academy under the name of a College, with its privileges and powers. Dr. Hill says, "that after the capture of Cornwallis and his army, the students returned to College, and Dr. Smith entered de novo, upon his various and responsible duties. The number of students continued to increase, until the rooms in the College were as full as they well could contain."

In 1789, Mr. Smith resigned the Presidency of the College, and gave himself entirely to the work of the ministry.*

For men of great magnitude and brightness to illumine the darkness of her colonial destitution, Virginia was greatly indebted to the Scotch Irish race of Pennsylvania, and the seminaries, under the care and teachings of their Presbyterian ministers, men of the same origin, or descent, being born or receiving their early education in Pennsylvania, which was afterwards pursued at the College of New Jersey, to the procurement of a Degree. This was followed by theological studies for the ministry, which obtained for them the license of a Presbytery, under whose care they were, and became missionaries to the south. Some of them were instrumental, with others, in establishing, in Virginia, a Seminary of learning, which afterwards became Washington College, at Lexington.

North Carolina, as an American colony, was early debtor to the Scotch Irish of Pennsylvania, for supplies by an elevated and pious ministry, to their destitute Presbyterian congregations, made up chiefly of emigrants from Ireland and Scotland, directly, and others from the same countries, after a residence, for a time, in Virginia or Pennsylvania. From the same source, was received their pioneers in the establishment of classical and scientific schools, for the education of the young men of the colony in the higher branches of knowledge.

Among the first, was the Rev. Hugh McAden, born in Pennsylvania, of Irish descent, a graduate of Nassau Hall, receiving his instruction in theology under the direction of the Rev. John Blair. He was licensed by the New Castle Presbytery,

* Dr. Foote's Sketches of Virginia, 406.

1755, in which year, as a missionary, he visited the Presbyterian settlements of North Carolina, and preached to many congregations, the first sermon they had heard in the colony. In 1759, being ordained, he accepted a pastoral charge in North Carolina, and labored faithfully, and acceptably for many years, till his death.

He was followed, in a few years, by the eminent and learned Rev. David Caldwell, D. D., who combined in himself the sound and pious minister of the Gospel, with the profound, accomplished and successful instructor of young men. He was born in Lancaster county, Pennsylvania, in 1725, and pursued his preparatory course of studies, under the tuition of the Rev. Robert Smith, of Pequea, in that county, distinguished for his usefulness, and as the father of sons, educated under his care, who were at the same time Presidents of the Colleges of New Jersey and Hampden Sidney. Mr. Caldwell graduated at Princeton, in 1761, where he engaged, for a time, as a Tutor and in the study of theology. Being licensed and ordained by the Presbytery of New Brunswick, he became a missionary to some vacant congregations in North Carolina, that had solicited supplies from the Synod of Philadelphia. In some of these congregations were acquaintances and friends, who, a few years before, had removed into that colony. In 1768, he accepted a pastoral charge there, and commenced a classical school, where he continued, until the infirmities of age disqualified him as a teacher. This school was the second classical school, of permanence, and perhaps the first in usefulness, in the upper part of Carolina. The instruction in this school, was thorough, and it flourished, being instrumental, during the long period of its continuance, in bringing more men into the learned professions, than any other taught by a single individual, or by a succession of teachers, during the same period of time. Five of his scholars became Governors of States, a number were promoted to high places in the Judiciary ; about fifty became ministers of the Gospel, and a large number were physicians and lawyers. He was of the most studious habits, his thoughts always exalted to the true dignity of his work, and where led by convictions of duty, and a desire to be useful, he was untiring in labor, persevering and inflexible from his purpose. Most, if not all, of his students, received their entire classical education from him, so that for a time, his school was Academy, College and Theological Seminary.*

"Living in the exciting times of the Revolution, with the royal army at his door, he was an ardent whig. So great was his influence, on the side of American Independence, that he became obnoxious to Lord Cornwallis, and his officers. Dr. Caldwell's residence was but a few miles from Guilford Court House, and his congregations were harassed by the plunderings, and cruelties of the needy and irritated army of Cornwallis, which were endured by a patriotic people with a constancy and bravery to be admired and held in grateful remembrance. The house of this eminent patriot and minister of the Gospel, on the Sabbath, was plundered, his wife and children turned out of doors, his property stolen, his library and valuable papers burned, by the royal army. A purse of £200 was set, by his Lordship, on the Doctor's head, to any one who would bring him in a prisoner. But the camp of General Green, saved him from the ferocious enemy.

The useful life of Dr. Caldwell, was prolonged by Providence, till August, 1824, when he departed this life at the age of ninety-nine years. His pastoral services were continued until 1820, his ninety-fourth year, requiring assistance, from weakness, on his return home, to dismount from his horse, and be carried into his house."

Others might be named, of Scotch Irish nativity, in Pennsylvania, who, after receiving an education in her Log Colleges, which was afterwards extended at Nassau Hall, Princeton, were missionaries of education as well as of the Gospel, to the Scotch Irish settlements of Virginia, North Carolina, and Tennessee, where their labors were blessed with extensive usefulness.

* It is a gratification to us, and the more so, as it is rare in these days, to find a descendant of the Puritans, as the Rev. W. Henry Foote, in his Sketches of North Carolina and Virginia, exhibit a spirit of liberality and justice to the Scotch Irish race, who form a large portion of the population of those States, and who for intelligence, integrity, patriotism, and religious character, have received, as they deserved, high commendation.

New Jersey was indebted, chiefly, to the founders and patrons of the Log Colleges of eastern Pennsylvania, for the establishment of the College of Nassau Hall, at Princeton, in the infancy of that colony, and which did more to distinguish and benefit it, than any other Institution ever created within its bounds. It was of Scotch Irish origin, and was nursed and fostered into great usefulness, and celebrity by the men of Irish and Scotch nativity, or descent, in Pennsylvania. Though in Maryland, Presbyterian congregations had been formed on the Eastern shore, as well as in Baltimore county, in the early part of the eighteenth century, yet they were small, and languished, as the influx of emigrants of that denomination would seem to have preferred other colonies for their settlements. Settlers, or citizens of enterprise, were attracted from the counties of Cumberland and Lancaster, Pennsylvania, in1760, to Baltimore town, then containing thirty or forty houses, and about three hundred inhabitants. These emigrants were Presbyterians of Irish or Scotch descent; they organized themselves into a congregation, and invited the Rev. Patrick Allison, as before briefly noticed, as a supply for one year. Mr. Allison was a native of Lancaster county, Pennsylvania, the son of Irish parents, and received his classical and preparatory education at the Philadelphia Academy, where he was engaged, for some time, as an assistant teacher.

Mr. Allison accepted the charge, and in 1765, was fully ordained to the pastoral office, by the Presbytery of Philadelphia. Mr. Allison was a man of learning, and piety. The matter of his sermons was rich and instructive, and his style clear and nervous. He was especially distinguished in the Church courts, and Dr. Miller has said of him, that in debate, he had scarce an equal. He died in 1802, having served this congregation nearly forty years. This congregation, from a little handful, that organized it, and called Mr. Allison, during his ministry, became one of the largest and most influential in the country. Mr. Allison was also prominent in every effort, in his day, to promote morality, education, and liberty in Maryland.

CHAPTER VI.

South Western Pennsylvania—Its early settlements—Controversy with Virginia as to Boundary—Purchase by Proprietary of Indian claim 1768—Open to appropriation by Pennsylvania grants after 1769—Influx of settlers restrained by apprehension of Indian hostilities, and war of Revolution—Boundary with Virginia settled by compact—Rapid progress after the Revolution—Missionaries—Supervision of Philadelphia and New York Synod—Messrs. Power McMillan, Smith, Dod, and others—Toil and sacrifices—Success in organization of Presbyterian congregations—Redstone Presbytery—Seminaries of learning—Public men: St. Clair, Brackenridge, Ross, Addison, Gallatin, Findlay—Western insurrection—Peace, and order—Literary and Theological institutions—Improvements and increase of population—Extent of district—Religion and morals of people.

THE great district of Pennsylvania, for the development of the Scotch Irish character, in its energies, enterprise, religious, and moral principles, as well as its educational tendencies and usefulness, was southwestern Pennsylvania.

The first settlements, by the whites, in Pennsylvania, west of the Allegheny mountains, on lands bordering on the Ohio, Monongahela, Youghiogeny, and Allegheny rivers, and their tributaries, were shortly before, and after Braddock's defeat, in 1755. These were chiefly under grants or permits from the Governor or authorities of the colony of Virginia, which claimed the country on these waters, embracing the locality of Pittsburg, then called Fort Duquesne, occupied by a French garrison. Some emigrants from Maryland had also settled in the same country.

Those who settled in that attractive and fertile district, un. der a claim of Pennsylvania jurisdiction, before 1769, did so in contravention of public law, as those lands had not been purchased by the Proprietary of Pennsylvania, from the Indians, until by the treaty at Fort Stanwix, in 1768, and were not open to purchase, settlement or appropriation, under the laws of Pennsylvania, until after that purchase.

Yet there were adventurous and restless spirits from Pennsylvania, and elsewhere, east of the Allegheny mountain, who, contrary to law, and in defiance of the Proclamation of the Governor of Pennsylvania, and public magistrates, presumed to make settlements, to a limited extent, in this western country, likely to be overrun by settlers claiming under Virginia. By that colony, and its authorities, the Indian claim was not regarded, and their laws allowed the grants to individuals, of land, in quantities, as desired, and at prices less than one tenth of that fixed by the Proprietary of Pennsylvania, as the price of vacant land within his province.

These settlements were in 1768, and shortly before the subject of complaints, by the western Indians, both to the Proprietary of Pennsylvania, as well as the Provincial government of that colony. A law of excessive severitv was passed by its Legislature in 1768, subjecting to *capital* punishment, the offence of a settlement on lands unpurchased by the Proprietary, from the Indian claimants. The Governor of Pennsylvania, in February, 1768, issued a Proclamation, requiring settlers to remove from these lands, informing them of the penalties to which they were subject, and appointed the Rev. John Steele, and others, of Cumberland county, commissioners, on behalf of the Government and Proprietary, to visit the settlements; carry with them and distribute the Proclamation; require the settlers to remove, and warn them of the consequences, if they did not, to themselves, from the Governor's prosecution and Indian hostilities. The commissioners proceeded at once to visit these settlements, for the purpose required, and in April, 1768, reported to the Governor, that there were but about one hundred and fifty families on the different settlements on Redstone, Youghiogeny and Cheat Rivers, which they visited, and made known the law, and requisitions of the government, but to little purpose, as respected the removal of the settlers, who generally were inclined to take their chances of hostilities from the Indians, with whom the Proprietary agents were understood, to be then negotiating, for the purchase of their claim to the lands on those waters. The requisitions of the Governor and the penalties of the law, seemed to have but had little regard, in the consideration of the settlers. The excessive severity of the law, rendered it inoperative. No one supposed, that the Government, or any authority under it, would attempt to carry into execution, a law, subjecting to the punishment of death a settler, for the offence of putting up a cabin for the residence of his family, and clearing and cultivating some fertile land, as the means of supporting that family, in an extensive wilderness, because an Indian tribe of hunters, living in their wigwams, at a distance of one hundred miles or more, made claim to half the Province, for their hunting ground, until they received some remuneration for their release. They did not consider their offence as *mala in se*, but as prohibited, from considerations of public policy, on which public sentiment was divided. The Governor of Virginia had, by proclamation, at the same time, required the removal of settlers under Virginia claims, from the disputed territory, but with no better success.

The settlers in the neighborhood of Fort Pitt, by the permission of George Croghan, superintendent of Indian affairs; and those who had settled on the main roads, leading across the mountains to Fort Pitt, by permits from the commanders and other officers of the army, for the convenience of the army, its reinforcements and supplies, were exempt from the penalties of the law, and the requisitions of the public magistrates.

The Indian claim being removed, by the purchase of the Proprietary, at Fort Stanwix, Nov. 5, 1768, these lands were open to settlement, grants or appropriations, under Pennsylvania, which now progressed more rapidly, though obstructed by interference of settlers under Virginia, and the uncertainty of title, in this conflict of jurisdiction between the two colonies. The settlements, however, were extended, in a country attractive for fertility of soil, with all the advantages of climate, water, and timber. Emigrants, from the east side of the mountains, could only reach it by a long journey, over lofty mountains, by rugged roads, scarcely passable for any wheel carriage, conveying their families on pack horses, with their supplies of clothing and bedding. Yet, before the Revolution, and pending that war, many families of subtance, intelligence, religious and moral character, overcame obstacles, which would seem insurmountable, in making their way to an abode, on the choice lands of south western Pennsylvania. When these adventurous and resolute emigrants, got to the end of their journey, it was to settle in the wilderness, with a log cabin for their dwelling; neighbors few and far between; separated from eastern friends and relatives by mountain ranges, a barrier to an interchange of visits, except at great intervals; without the comforts and conveniences enjoyed by eastern friends, and remote from all seminaries of education, and where the worship of their heavenly Father, by an assembled congregation, was in the open air, with the firmament for a canopy, and for their seats, the bare earth, or the rough logs of the forest.

These settlements, during the Revolutionary war, and for years after, were exposed to the hostilities of the Indians, who, frequently, by their stealthy marches, surprised and alarmed the inhabitants, often marking their way by fire, and the massacre of families. The conflict of jurisdiction between the two States, in the exercise of the powers of government, obstructed the administration of justice, incommoded the inhabitants, and led to contests and arrests, between the officers of these border States, that were harassing to both.

In 1779, the States of Pennsylvania and Virginia, agreed to terminate this unprofitable controversy, by an extension of the Mason and Dixon line west, as a boundary, saving to all persons previously acquired rights, under the laws and usages of these States, according to priority, which was executed and ratified. By the boundary provided for and established, the large district of fine country in dispute between Virginia and Pennsylvania, was permanently assigned to Pennsylvania, as her territory.

The early settlers, who had settled within this district, under either of these governments, were, with few exceptions, of Irish and Scotch nativity or descent. Having a common origin, and associations, they were much alike in principles and habits, agreeing in their religious professions and doctrines, devoted to the principles of the Protestant reformation, choosing and maintaining the Presbyterian church organization, as that most approved by them. Amongst these Presbyterians, there were some slight shades of difference, to separate them, chiefly on Psalmody, which led to the organization of separate and distinct ecclesiastical judicatories, that are yet maintained, though agreeing in having a common standard of doctrine and creed, as well as of church government, contained in the Westminster Confession of Faith, with its Church rules and Catechisms.

The Synod of Philadelphia and New York did not overlook the settlers, who had taken up their abode in the wilderness, west of the Allegheny, and at an early day provision was made by them to have these distant settlements on the frontiers supplied with suitable and qualified missionaries, licensed and ordained by the Presbytery to the work of the ministry. In 1766, the Rev. Charles Beaty, of Irish nativity, who had obtained his classical education in Ireland, before his emigration, pursued his studies, with a view to the Gospel ministry, at the Log College, at Neshaminy, then under the care of the celebrated Wm. Tennent, and was licensed by the Presbytery of New Brunswick. He was associated with Rev. G. Duffield, a minister of high reputation and experience, to visit the frontier settlement of the far west region, as well as the Indians, as missionaries, by the appointment of the Synod.

These appointments were continued, by this Synod, from time to time, through a series of twenty years, to supply the destitute brethren on the south western frontier of Pennsylvania and Virginia, with not only accredited missionaries, but of a high order for talents, learning, piety and experience in the ministry. Their labors in preaching, catechising, and administering the ordinances of the Church, were blessed, in organizing congregations amongst the settlers for the maintenance of Christian worship, and religious instruction, training and government.

Messrs. Beaty and Duffield, owing to the apprehension of Indian disturbances, were enabled only to visit some of the settlements, and the missions were afterwards renewed, extended and fulfilled, by the labors of Rev. James Finley, and others, under the appointments of the Presbyteries of New Castle and Donegal.

The first ordained minister, that settled with his family, in Western Pennsylvania, was the Rev. James Power, D. D. He was born in Chester county, Pennsylvania, the child of pious parents, who had emigrated from the north of Ireland. His education, preparatory to entering College, is believed to have been at the Fagg's manor school, of that county, under the care of the eminent Rev. John Blair. He graduated at Nassau Hall, Princeton, in 1766, and was licensed by the Presbytery of New Castle in 1772. He labored for several years as a missionary, in the western settlements, as well as in Virginia. In the summer of 1776, in the exciting times of the Revolution, and when the country was most agitated with the question of Independence, Mr. Power decided upon going west with his family, and he was ordained for that purpose at Octararo, Lancaster county. In the autumn of that year, he removed, with his family, and took up his residence in the bounds of Dunlap's creek congregation, which is within the county of Fayette. Mr. Power labored, after his removal to the west, to supply the destitute churches, over an extensive district, though he resided at Dunlap's creek, the principal place of his labors, and not until 1779, he became the regular pastor of Sewickly and Mount Pleasant congregations. He lived to the age of eighty-five, greatly venerated and beloved for his piety, fidelity, and usefulness. "He was a graceful speaker, and of polished manners. His sermons were clear, methodical and expressive in language, well selected. His enunciation was so perfect, that when he spoke in the open air, as he frequently did, he could be heard at a great distance. His ministry was successful in edifying Christians, instructing the young and improving the morals of the community." Such was the man of Irish parentage, educated in the schools of the Scotch Irish ministers, that turned his back on the comforts of more refined society, and this world's enjoyments and emoluments, in the older settlements, east of the mountains, and became the first settled minister in the bounds of the old Redstone Presbytery.

The great pioneer of evangelical and practical religion, as well as of improved education in western Pennsylvania, was the Rev. John McMillan, D. D., born in Fagg's manor, Chester county, Pennsylvania, in 1752, the child of Irish parents. His classical education was acquired at his native place, in the academy under the care and direction of the Rev. John Blair, distinguished for talents and learning, as well as for the eminence of many of his pupils, in learning, eloquence and piety. Mr. McMillan finished his classical studies under the Rev. Robert Smith, at Pequea, and entered Princeton College in 1770. He graduated in 1772 and returning to Pequea to pursue his study of theology, under Dr. Robert Smith, was licensed by the Presbytery of New Castle, in 1774. He early exhibited his missionary zeal, and under appointments, visited vacant congregations of Presbyterians, in the valley of Virginia, also in western Pennsylvania. Though his talents, learning, piety, and other qualifications, for an acceptable and qualified minister, would have commanded the most comfortable situation in the Church, in the old settlements, yet, Mr. McMillan chose to forego all these, traverse the great wilderness of mountains, and cast his lot and that of his family, with the settlers, on the waters of the Monongahela and Youghiogeny, with all the sacrifices, privations, toils, sufferings, and perils, that were attendant upon these remote settlements, destitute of the comforts and conveniences of social life, as well as of ministerial labors, teaching, and Gospel ordinances. He was ordained by the Presbytery of Donegal, at Chambersburg, June, 1776. The Revolutionary movements and Indian disturbances, prevented him from removing his family at once, though he visited the congregations of Chartiers and Pigeon creek, in western Pennsylvania, as often as circumstances would allow, and to his new field of labor in these congregations, as a settled pastor, he brought his family in November, 1778. We are furnished with his own account of the new residence he had for himself and family, in the new field of labor he had chosen for his abode, and that of his family.*

The leadings of Providence would seem to be marked and observable in the destiny, and labors, of this eminent minister of the Gospel, and instructor. The times, the state of the country, and people, to whom he went, required no ordinary man, but one of uncommon energy, resolution, industry and perseverance, with ability, learning, sound in the faith, of practical piety; apt to teach and willing to spend his powers and be spent, in the service of his Divine Master. The Rev. Mr. McMillan was the man for this service. Not discouraged by the untoward circumstances of his new residence, in his log cabin of simple structure, and plain accommodation for his family, he entered on his pastoral labors with zeal. The circumstances in which he was placed, required him to "work with his own hands," in handling the axe, and the other implements of the sturdy laborer, in the new country. He was of vigorous bodily powers, and during his long life, was never confined half a day by sickness.

"Though it was necessary for him to labor in improving his building and clearing his land, he did not allow this to inter-

* Dr. McMillan, in a letter to Dr. Carnahan, in 1832, gave the following account of his arrival in this western field, in 1778. [Old Redstone. 186.]

"When I came to this country, the cabin in which I was to live, was raised, but there was no roof to it, nor any chimney or floor. The people, however, were very kind, they assisted me in preparing my house, and on the 16th of December, I removed into it. But we had neither bedstead, nor tables, nor stool, nor chair, nor bucket. All these things we had to leave behind us, as there was no wagon road at that time over the mountains, we could bring nothing with us but what was carried on pack horses. We placed two boxes one on the other, which served us for a table, and two kegs served us for seats, and having committed ourselves to God, in family worship, we spread a bed on the floor and slept soundly till morning. The next day, a neighbor coming to my assistance, we made a table and stool, and in a little time, had every thing comfortable about us. Sometimes, indeed, we had no bread for weeks together, but we had plenty of pumpkins and potatoes, and all the necessaries of life; as for luxuries, we were not much concerned about them. We enjoyed health, the gospel and its ordinances and pious friends. We were in the place where we believed God would have us to be; and we did not doubt, but that He would provide every thing necessarv; and glory to his name, we were not disappointed."

He was a man of vigorous bodily powers, and could endure labor or toil with any of his neighbors. On one occasion, having made appointments to preach at two places, and his horse having strayed away, he proceeded on foot, and fulfilled his appointments, by preaching at both places, and walking in all, seventeen miles for the purpose, on the Sabbath.

fere with his more important duties, as a minister of the Gospel, to which he gave all the energies of his body and mind."

This great father of the Presbyterian Church, in the west, was not content with doctrinal and practical religious instruction and pastoral visitation, to the people of his several pastoral charges, but at an early period after his removal to the west, in imitation of the log colleges of eastern Pennsylvania, and with the example before him of the Principals of those Seminaries, where he received his education, and training, he directed his attention to the establishment, in the western wilds, of a Log College, for the education of young men in the higher branches of education, as well as of preparation of those of piety for the ministry. Like the Tennents, Blairs, Smith, and others, he erected near his own dwelling, a log building, of which he was to be the principal and instructor of young men.

Among the early and eminent ministers and teachers, who penetrated into western Pennsylvania, was the Rev. Thaddeus Dod, from New Jersey, a licentiate of the Presbytery of New York. He removed to the Redstone settlement in 1778, taking up his abode at Fort Lenalley, on the border of what is now Virginia. The Fort was a place of shelter and defence, to the inhabitants of the settlement, against the Indian incursions, then frequent and alarming. His first preaching and administering the ordinance of baptism, was within the Fort. The locality was the most perilous from Indian warfare, of any place in western Pennsylvania. Mr. Dod settled on a farm, in the neighborhood, and after a few years, a "meeting house" of hewn logs, was built near the Fort. He possessed a highly cultivated and well disciplined mind. "His power of concentration, and of holding his thoughts closely upon any point, or subject of investigation, amidst any amount of external interruption, was perhaps never exceeded." Not only was he an accurate classical scholar, thoroughly versed in the Latin, Greek and Hebrew languages, but a profound mathematician. Soon after his settlement in the west, he united with his great office of preaching the Gospel, the office of instructor of youth, in the higher branches of classical and scientific education. The settlers of this neighborhood, in 1781, united in putting up a

Log Academy. It would appear, from historical records, that Mr. Dod was the first in his efforts, in this wild country, to promote the cause of education. His pastoral charge was large, and received his faithful and diligent attention. In 1789, he was appointed first Principal of Washington Academy, at Washington, Pa., which, in 1806, was merged into Washington College. The burning of the building in which this Academy was conducted, induced Mr. Dod to return to his first field of labor, where he died in 1793. His pupils held him in the highest respect, and "he had the happy faculty of infusing into those who were capable of it, an intense love of science and literature." When his various traits of character are considered, and the remarkable combination of talents found in him, all must admire the Providential dispensation that assigned to such a man, so useful and responsible, but yet perilous and self-denying charge.

Amongst his first scholars, were the Rev. James Hughes, John Brice, James McGready, Samuel Porter, and Thomas Marshall, men of talent, piety, and usefulness in the ministry. The efforts of Rev. Mr. Dod, and Dr. Smith, in that western region, in education, may have preceded those of Dr. McMillan a short time; and it would appear, that many young men, who had been studying under their direction, afterwards placed themselves under the instruction of Dr. McMillan, as to their literary course, as well as their theological instruction. Dr. McMillan was the great patron of the Academy founded at Canonsburg, in 1792, and when it became a chartered College, it had, in him, a steady and faithful friend, throughout his life. For many years after his settlement in the west, he and his family were exposed to great privations and trials, and sometimes to such peril from the Indian enemy, as to compel them to seek shelter in the Fort. His ministerial labors were arduous, and greatly blessed. It is said, by a biographer, who knew him well, the late Rev. Dr. M. Brown, "that it was supposed that hundreds and even thousands, were, through his instrumentality, converted and trained up for heaven, and that perhaps one hundred ministers were trained, more or less, in his school of the prophets, many of whom were eminently useful."

He preached often, in 1833, the year of his death, in the eighty-second year of his age, and sixtieth of his ministry, on some occasions leaning on a crutch for the support of his aged frame.*

The Rev. Joseph Smith, was an able coadjutor of Dr. McMillan and Rev. James Power, D. D., in the great western field of ministerial labor. He had graduated at Princeton in 1762, and was licensed by the Presbytery of New Castle, to preach the Gospel in 1767. After laboring for some years in the eastern settlements, and visiting the west, he accepted of a call from Cross creek and Buffalo, in western Pennsylvania. In 1780, he moved into the bounds of the latter, as their pastor. "He was a thorough classical scholar, of well disciplined mind, sound in the faith, abounding in piety and zeal in his ministerial work, in which his labors, as a pastor, were eminently blessed, and though preaching was his great work, he was distinguished for his usefulness out of the pulpit, in catechetical instruction of the young, and in his earnest and affective conversation with his people about their eternal interests."

The first school that was opened in the west, for training young men for the sacred office of the ministry, was begun by Mr. Smith, at Buffalo, Washington county, Pennsylvania, about 1785. Mr. Smith had a small building erected in a corner of his garden, called "the students' room." In this, and the log cabin of Dr. McMillan, were educated in the west some men who were distinguished for their influence and usefulness in society, and in the Church. Amongst these were the Rev. Messrs. William Swan, Samuel Porter, James Hughes, John Brice, David Smith, Joseph Patterson. The school for the languages and sciences was continued for some time, and then, by some mutual arrangement, was transferred, and or-

* In the grave yard of Charteirs, over his remains, is erected by the congregation, a tomb-stone, the following, is a part of the inscription : "Erected in memory of the Rev. John McMillan, D. D., an able divine, a preacher of the first order. His distinguished talents, his active benevolence, his private virtue, his exalted piety, the skill and ability which he displayed in instructing, and training young men for the Gospel ministry, his indefatigable zeal in promoting his Master's cause, and the best interests of his fellow-men, have raised a monument to his fame, far more imperishable than the stone which bears this inscription. He was the leading founder of Jefferson College."

ganized near Canonsburg, under the care of Dr. McMillan, and out of which was raised Jefferson College.

The first Presbytery, organized in western Pennsylvania was, in September, 1781, by the Rev. Messrs. John McMillan, James Power, and Thaddeus Dod, with their elders; the Rev. Joseph Smith, being absent. It was called "the Presbytery of Redstone." The term "Redstone settlement," designated most of the country in south western Pennsylvania, claimed by Pennsylvania or Virginia, embracing what now constitutes the counties of Fayette, Washington, Green, and parts of Westmoreland, and Allegheny. The settlement took its name from that of a creek, which enters the Monongahela near Brownsville, a place of ancient notoriety, by the name of "Redstone old Fort."

The influx of emigrants, after the Revolution, was rapid, and continued from eastern Pennsylvania, as well as from Virginia, with a considerable number direct from Ireland. The great mass were of Irish nativity, or descent, and members of the Presbyterian Church.

Amongst them were adventurers, of coarse and uncultivated habits, ignorant and disorderly, looking to the chase for their pastime and occupation; and content with a rude cabin, and a small patch of land for cultivation, to which there was no great attachment, when anything more advantageous, in the country presented itself, as an inducement to a removal. There were, however, as stated by reliable historians, in this western settlement, at the close of the Revolutionary war, and after, "a numerous class of persons, possessing a degree of refinement and intelligence, that would have no occasion to blush in the presence of any class of persons, native or otherwise, now to be found amongst us. Many of them continued to gather around them some of the usual appendages of a higher social life. Throughout a portion of Westmoreland, Fayette and Washington counties, there were many gentlemen farmers of refined, easy manners, courtly in their address, social and hospitable, always ready to receive the ministers on their weary journey to distant meetings, or to the destitute settlements." Thus with this class of families seated around them through their respective fields of labor, the Presbyterian ministers were greatly aided in their efforts for the general improvement of the domestic and social state of the country." In addition to this class, "there were amongst these settlers of the west, a still more numerous one, of plain, substantial, Scotch Irish people, who, though somewhat blunt and unpolished in their manners, yet for real kindness of disposition, integrity and hospitality, were not excelled by any of their descendants."

Too much praise cannot be bestowed upon the female sex of this middle class. There was a great energy of character, a patient endurance of the hardships of frontier life, and a cheerful submission to domestic privations, which entitle them to the grateful remembrance of the present generation." [Old Redstone by Dr. Smith, 109.]

It must be admitted by every candid inquirer, that the debt of gratitude owing by the western country, to the four missionary pioneers of south western Pennsylvania, was an immense one ; and which we, at this distant day, are unable to compute. Their memories should be regarded with reverence, as the great benefactors of their age. Men of talents and education, commissioned by the courts of the Church to preach the everlasting Gospel, to their fellow-men, burning with missionary spirit and zeal, sought the destitute settlements of our western frontier, as the field of their labor. They were not held back by the superior comforts, associations and refinements of society, east of the mountain ranges, but with their families, at their own expense, traversed a wilderness of mountains, by the traders' or Indians' path, with toil, privations, and fatigue, insurmountable to all but men and women of uncommon energy, and resolution, to be engaged in a good work. This great western field was only to be reached and occupied, at the peril of health and life, from exposure in a country of almost unbroken forest, and with savage enemies roaming from time to time through its fastnesses, to way-lay, surprise and often massacre defenceless families. An overuling Providence directed their way, watched over, and guarded them and their families, on their perilous journey, and conducted them safely to the places of their destination on the frontier settlements. When there, the same Almighty care was over them, to guard, and bless them in their labors in behalf of their fellow-men. Though laboring in season and out of season, their service in the work of their Divine Master was to them all, one of many years, and the two Messrs. Power and McMillan, who would seem to have first entered the service, had their lives prolonged to four score years and upwards. They were allowed to live to see their work prosper, and the fruits of their labors, in an extended and flourishing Church, an educated and elevated ministry, and the pupils of their seminaries adorning the learned professions, and the halls of legislation, with men of education, learning, and usefulness. There was in the lives of these apostles to the frontier, an exalted manifestation of disinterestedness, and personal sacrifice seldom equalled. They were the great instruments to promote the religious, moral and intellectual improvement of large and rapidly increasing settlements of American freemen and their families, and in elevating them to a degree in the scale of intelligence, refinement, enterprise, elevated Christian principle, and every virtue and quality, with the most favored communities of our great Commonwealth.

The Rev. Mr. Doddridge, an Episcopal clergyman of estimation in western Virginia, and author of a work on the life and manners of the western settlers, states: "That the ministry of the Gospel has contributed, no doubt, immensely to the happy change which has been effected in the state of our western society. At an early period of our settlements, three Presbyterian clergymen commenced their clerical labors in our infant settlements: Rev. Joseph Smith, Rev. John McMillan and the Rev. James Power. They were pious, patient, laborious men, who collected their people into regular congregations, and did for them all that their circumstances would allow. It was no disparagement to them that their first churches were the shady groves, and their first pulpits a kind of tent, constructed of a few rough slabs, covered with clapboards. He who dwelleth not exclusively in temples made with hands, was propitious to their devotions." After referring, with approbation, to the grammar schools, established at their own houses, or in their immediate neighborhoods, he bears his testimony to their success and usefulness, in establishing, first, Canonsburg Academy, incorporated into Jefferson College, he says: "This institution has been remarkably successful in its operations. It has produced a large number of good scholars, in all the literary professions, and added immensely to the science of the country. Next to this, Washington College has been the means of diffusing much of the light of science through the western country. Too much praise cannot be bestowed on these good men, who opened these fruitful sources of instruction for our infant country, at so early a period of its settlement. They have immensely improved the departments of theology, law, medicine, and legislation in the western regions."

This is impartial and high testimony, from a respectable and intelligent minister of another Christian denomination, to the character and usefulness of the Presbyterian ministers of the Scotch Irish race, who at an early day, entered western Pennsylvania, when a wilderness, and whose labors and success were in the neighborhood of the dwelling of Mr. Doddridge, and of which he was for many years an observer.

The usages of our State and National Governments have been, to accord for public services, to some of the distinguished actors in the land and naval armaments, their honors, and rewards, by the resolutions of their legislative bodies, by votes of thanks, medals or swords. And sometimes the people, by the highest gift in their power, have elevated to the Presidency of the Republic, a successful General, with little regard to qualification for the office of Chief Magistrate of a constitutional government. Where death has conquered the conqueror of a host of his fellow-men by their slaughter, or captivity, there has been erected to his memory a monument of marble or bronze, to commemorate his deeds of human carnage.

The benefactors of their age, by deeds of philanthrophy, by their labors of love, in the religious, moral, and intellectual improvement of great communities of the people, over extensive districts of the country, unprovided for by the government, are left only to the spontaneous effusions and gratitude of individuals, or the communities, specially favored by their labors.

What is there, in a Christian country, to elevate a military chieftain in public favor, above the faithful missionary in the service of the King of kings? The military commander, in his march to the seat of war, when on the frontier, has his accompaniments of soldiers, to pitch and strike his tent, have the care of his horse and baggage, protect his person, minister to his wants, and execute his orders, and when he reaches the country of the enemy, his toil, exposure and peril are often ended by a campaign of a few months, or a single battle, in which the fortunes of war, superior numbers, or military tactics, had given him a victory, to be applauded by his all-observing countrymen.

It is to be deplored, that the tendencies of public sentiment, in our great Republic, should be so much to create a war spirit, foster and honor military prowess, place it in the front rank of public service, and make war and the army the high road to honor and distinction. The organization of our government is adapted to peace, with the progress and prosperity that are the growth of peaceful relations. War is not the element for its success and permanency, but should be considered and averted as a great calamity to the nation, unless, when national honor and safety impose it.

The missionary of the Gospel of peace, is a soldier of the cross, whose weapon is the sword of the Spirit, with the Bible for his shield and banner. His war is with ignorance, vice, sin and infidelity; the conquest sought by him is not one of blood or death, but to bring all the enemies of God and man captive from death unto life, and from sin unto righteousness. His energy, fortitude, bravery, and zeal, are attested by toil, and exposure of life, not only in his solitary and perilous journeys in the country, traversed by savage enemies, or in the campaign of one season, or a single battle field, but by a long life of faithful and devoted service to his Divine Master. His reward is the satisfaction of doing that Master's work on earth, and he may hope for the recompense of reward to a faithful servant in the life to come, from the righteous Judge of the living and the dead.

Ministers Plenipotentiary have been appointed from time to

time, and sent, by our national government, with expensive outfits and salaries, to represent it in its foreign relations, to the European governments of the highest rank; and on some occasions, they have been honored with a passage across the ocean in a national ship; and after living sumptuously, and enjoying the society of royalty, and nobility, for some years, returned to their country, and yet how few of these public characters, in all their diplomacy, have rendered to the welfare and prosperity of their country, a *tithe* of the benefits rendered by more than one of the Presbyterian ministers named, in the mission from the Church, to the frontier settlements of western Pennsylvania, by their labor and services in extending religious and moral influence, and diffusing and elevating education.

After the Revolutionary war was ended, and peace established, the emigration to western Pennsylvania increased rapidly. The district of country, embracing the present counties of Westmoreland, Fayette, Allegheny, Washington and Green, was attractive to settlers from the counties of Chester, Lancaster, York and Cumberland. Many of these were emigrants from Ireland, who had taken up their residence for a time, in the eastern part of the State, where they had sojourned, with their friends, or countrymen. Many emigrants also, as they arrived from Ireland, directed their way to the Scotch Irish settlements, rapidly progressing, in south western Pensylvania. The mass of these, were men of intelligence, resolution, energy, religious and moral character, having means that enabled them to supply themselves with suitable selections of land, for their residence and farm, and with the necessary stock and implements, for their accommodation. They were like their predecessors, east of the mountains, agriculturists of substance and industry, who sought a place for the permanent abode of their families, and the means of supporting them.

It is matter of some surprise, that so many substantial and respectable settlers, were attracted to such a residence at that time, west of the mountains, when there was so much land uncultivated in the Kittochtinny valley, and other valleys, east of the Allegheny mountain, that were equally fertile, and so much more accessible, and more convenient to the eastern settlements, and markets, as well as the land and other public offices, of the State government. These lands were to be purchased from individual holders, at moderate advances on the land office prices. We must suppose, that they had friends and relatives, who had preceded them, to the western waters, whose association and neighborhood they preferred, and whose description of the country of their settlement, and its fresh and fertile soil, had in it much to attract them. We cannot say, at this day, they acted unwisely, or that their circumstances and those of their familes, would have been improved by a residence east of the Allegheny mountain. The resolution, energy, enterprise and industry, that enabled them to overcome the obstacles of a journey across the mountain ranges, and the toils, sacrifices, and perils, incident to settlements so remote from market and more advanced communities, as well as from government aid and protection, formed in the men and women of those times, the characters most desirable and useful in this new and opening country, whose labors and perseverance converted the wilderness into well cultivated farms, constituted a barrier to savage incursions on the eastern settlements, organized congregations of Christian worshippers, and established and maintained schools and seminaries of education. The activity and character of such a population, were not to end with the one generation. It was transmissible to descendants, who had been brought up under such training and education, as made them, in after times, the great pioneers and founders of settlements of the northwestern territory and the States formed out of it, in which these descendants of the Scotch Irish settlers of western Pennsylvanla, were amongst the most prominent, useful, and distinguished citizens of the Republic.

These settlers are not to be confounded with rambling settlers, who were generally in advance of civilization, and on the confines of the frontier, and who made their hasty settlement without office grant or right, putting up a rough cabin, as a shelter for their families, attached to which, was a small patch of clear land, for the cultivation of some garden vegetables and corn, depending on their guns for supply of meat for their families, and for the skins and furs, that furnished them some of their clothing and household articles, and were their staples for sale or barter to the trader. This class of adventurers, who were, it is believed, more numerous on the confines of Virginia, and adjacent, and who have been graphically described by the Rev. Mr. Doddridge, in his published notes, on their habits, condition, and education, were little better than the Indians, and were ready to sell the preemption, or inception of title, under their improvement, to some settler of more means, and of different habits and character, who was able and willing to pay the squatter an advance on his improvement, and take from the land office an official grant, predicated on the improvement, as the inception of title. The improver, or squatter, thus selling, was ready, on short notice, to gather up his small stock of goods and chattles, and from his knowledge of the great extent of unimproved lands, in the country where he was accustomed to roam in pursuit of game, or his Indian foes, would set himself down on some other eligible tract of vacant land, and prosecute anew his speculating and roving propensities, by erecting the small log cabin, to be occupied until it might, in time, be sold to advantage, to some exploring emigrant, who was willing to purchase the possessory right to be confirmed by an official grant from the State, on the established terms of the law.

Settlers of the same character are to be found, in these days, on the frontier of the United States, intruding on the public lands, as well as those of Indian reservation, before they are open to appropriation and sale. They claim a preemption, when the lands are offered for sale by the government, and intimidate all competition of purchasers, by threats of violence and bloodshed, which are sometimes put into barbarous execution. They generally profess a willingness to sell out their preemption, which is often only a wrongful possession against law, and maintained in violation of law, but to which peaceful and orderly settlers are, for peace and safety, forced to submit. After sale, the roaming settler will renew and pursue his squatting propensities and uncivilized habits, in some more remote territory.

Amongst the emigrants that removed to western Pennsylvania, after the Revolutionary war, were ministers of the

Gospel in the Presbyterian Church, educated in the Log Colleges of eastern Pennsylvania, and graduates of Princeton College. Amongst these, was the Rev. James Finley, of Irish nativity, educated in his classical studies at the Log College, under the Rev. Samuel Blair, where he was trained to an accurate scholarship in the languages. He was the brother of Dr. Finley, President of Princeton College. The Rev. James Finley removed to the Forks of Youghiogeny, in western Pennsylvania, in 1783, where he was called and settled as a pastor in the Presbyterian Church. He had been licensed as a minister and officiated as such, for some years before, in eastern Pennsylvania, and had visited the Presbyterian congregations of west Pennsylvania, some years before his removal, to reside in that country. He was a man of eminent piety, and a devoted, faithful and excellent pastor.

The Rev. James Dunlap, a native of Chester county, Pennsylvania, receiving his early education in the schools of his neighborhood, graduated at Princeton College in 1773. He studied divinity under the Rev. James Finley, at east Nottingham, before his removal to the west; was licensed by the Presbytery of Donegal about 1781 ; ordained, *sine titulo*, by the Presbytery of New Castle, at Fagg's manor, in 1781, and shortly after removed to western Pennsylvania, where he was installed pastor of the Congregations of Laurel Hill and Dunlap's creek. In 1803, he was chosen President of Jefferson College, a station which he held with great respect until 1811, having had conferred on him the title of Doctor of Divinity, by the Trustees of the College, with which he was connected. He was represented as a man of great piety, and eminent for his accurate attainments in classical literature, with which it is said, he was so familiar, as to have the ancient classics in his memory, to recite, or hear and correct the recital of others.

There were several other ministers of the Presbyterian Church, educated in the Log Colleges of eastern Pennsylvania, some of whom graduated at Princeton College, directed their way, about the same time, to western Pennsylvania, as a field for their labor and services, and where their labors were greatly blessed and successful. This great district of country, embracing now six or more counties of distinction, wealth and influence in the State, would seem to have been peculiarly attractive to all classes of citizens, at an early day, many of whom, were eminent for talents, intelligence, learning, and usefulness. They disregarded the want of political, commercial, and social advantages, as enjoyed in eastern Pennsylvania, and would seem to have anticipated the improvements, that were to overcome the mountain barriers, and place them nearer to their State Capitol, as well as the seat of the National Government, eastern markets, and eastern associations.

Amongst these was Arthur St. Clair, of Scotch nativity, who, as a military commander, settled at Fort Ligonier, where he was, at the organization of Westmoreland county, in 1773, of the Courts of which, he was appointed the first Clerk. Though esteemed for military talents of an high order, bravery, integrity, and patriotism, which elevated him to the rank of Major General in the army of the American colonies, yet misfortune marked him as her own, and his memorable defeat by the Indians, has always been regarded as a sad event in the history of the Republic, imputable more to the condition and supplies of the army, than want of Generalship, in the commander, who, at the time, was helpless in his tent, from disease, and not able to mount his horse without assistance. Having served his country in many civil offices, with ability and fidelity, he died in Westmoreland county, in 1818, at the age of 84.

Hugh Henry Brackenridge, of high reputation, as a scholar, lawyer, politician and jurist in Pennsylvania, removed to western Pennsylvania, about 1781, as a place for his permanent abode. Having been brought by his parents from Scotland to York county, Pennsylvania, when he was a child; his early education was in the schools of his neighborhood, and pursued at Princeton College, where he graduated. He was licensed in the ministry of the Presbyterian Church, and served in the American army as a chaplain. Having relinquished the ministry, and studied law, he entered on its practice in western Pennsylvania, when that country was little more than a wilderness. In his profession, he was prosperous, and distinguished.

In 1800 he was appointed a Judge of the Supreme Court of the State, a station which he filled with ability, and which he retained until his death, in 1818.

James Ross, of Pittsburg, eminent for talents and learning, and distinguished as a lawyer, advocate and statesman, emigrated, a young man, from the *Barrens* of York county, to western Pennsylvania, shortly after the revolutionary war. He was a descendant of Scotch Irish parents, who had given him the plain education their circumstances and neighborhood afforded. By application, he advanced himself in his education, and for some time, was employed as a teacher. By pursuing his studies, he soon qualified himself for admission to the bar. His great powers of mind, with industry and application, gave him a rank, as a lawyer, that had few equals, and as a member of the Pennsylvania State Convention, to form a Constitution for its government, and as a statesman, in the United States Senate, he was not surpassed. His high and merited reputation, made him a public man of celebrity, in Pennsylvania, and of much regard in other States.

Alexander Addison, a Scotchman by birth, and education, was licensed as a minister, by a Presbytery of Scotland, and emigrated to the United States. He took up his abode in Washington county, Pennsylvania, in 1784, as a Presbyterian minister. As such, he officiated there acceptably, to the Presbyterian congregation in Washington, for some time, and they were desirous of having him for their permanent pastor. Mr. Addison there gave his attention to the study of the law, and withdrawing from the ministry, was admitted as an attorney of the Courts. His talents and superior acquirements, soon commanded attention and regard. In 1791, he was appointed the first President Judge of the Judicial District for that section of the State. He was a man of strong mind, great attainments, and undoubted integrity. His judicial opinions and charges to the Grand Juries of his District, are monuments of his sound judgment, legal learning, and political wisdom, as well as of his devotion to the peace, and good order of society, and the maintenance of the constitution and laws. Presiding at a time of great party excitement, and in a district where there was an organized, unlawful, but popular opposition, to some of the laws, and constituted authorities of the national government, he made himself obnoxious to the factious multitudes, by his conservative principles, and the exercise of his judicial powers in the preservation of order, and submission to the laws of the government. He was somewhat impatient in temper, and could not be courteous to ignorance, combined with rudeness and presumption.

Though impeached, and removed from his judicial station by a partisan Legislature of Pennsylvania, for frivolous cause, that did not impeach his integrity, he was dishonored less, in the estimation of a virtuous and intelligent community, than the public body, which unjustly sought to make him a victim to party persecution, and individual hostility.*

Albert Gallatin, a Swiss young man of talents and learning, who had graduated at Geneva, in Switzerland, sought a home in the American republic, and after visitlng several parts of the United States, between 1783 and 1785, by the advice of his friends, selected a place on the banks of the Monongahela, within the present county of Fayette, Pennsylvania, for his residence. As soon as he became known in that humble retirement, his talents and acquirements obtained for him the public respect and confidence. As early as 1789, he was elected, from the district of his residence, a member of the Convention to amend the Constitution of Pennsylvania, which brought him to public notice, as a man of abilities and learning. His subsequent life was one of official service, in the highest stations in the gift of the people, or in the appointment of the government, with the exception of the Presidency. His abilities, as a statesman, financier, and diplomatist, were acknowledged by the country, and are familiar to all who are conversant with the history of our government.

William Findlay, of the county of Westmoreland, settled in that county about the close of the Revolutionary war. He was an emigrant from Ireland, who had first settled on the

* "Alexander Addison was the President of the Courts in four counties, and I venture to say, that a more intelligent, learned, upright and fearless Judge was not to be found in the State." [Dr. Carnahan.]

Conococheague, in the Kittochtinny valley, about 1764. His means were small, and he there followed the humble occupation of a weaver. He was of limited early education, but of strong intellect, which he cultivated by reading and reflection. He acquired a knowledge of history and government, which made him an active and influential member of society, in its relations, and in all public measures. As a public man, he was respected for sagacity, experience and judgment. The confidence of the community, in his patriotism and judgment, was manifested where he resided, by his selection as one of the Council of Censors of the State government under the Constitution of 1776. He was a member of the Convention that formed the Constitution of 1790, and represented the district in which he resided, in other official stations of distinction and responsibility.

Scotch Irish families moved to this western district, during and immediately after, the Revolutionary war, in great numbers. In these families, were members, who united piety with intelligence, and a desire to cultivate their minds, and who, under the teachings and direction of the Rev. Messrs. Smith, McMillan, and Dod, qualified themselves, by their studies, for the ministry, to which, after proper probation and trial, they were admitted. Many of them were distinguished for ability and learning, as well as their aptness to teach, and their faithful devotion and labor as pastors; amongst whom, were the Rev. Joseph Patterson, Rev. Samuel Porter, Rev. Robert Marshall, of Irish nativity, Rev. James Hughes, Rev. John Brice, Rev. James McGready, Rev. Elisha McCurdy, of Irish descent, and others.

The praise of these men is still in the congregations, in which they were ministers, laboring faithfully, acceptably, and usefully. To these were added many other Presbyterian ministers of education, learning and piety, from the eastern part of the State, licensed by the Presbyteries of Donegal and Carlisle. We cannot give a sketch of their usefulness and labors, without extending this article beyond our proper limits.*

* The reader is referred, for full and very interesting information, respecting the incidents of their lives, in this western field, to Dr. Elliot's life of McCurdy, and others, and to "Old Redstone," by Dr. Smith.

In this western country, there were, at the close of the last century, and immediately before, a large amount of intelligence, with religious and moral character, as well as means and opportunities of literary, scientific, and theological education for young men, who would seek it, not as a pastime, for a portion of their life, but to be seduously improved to the acquisition of knowledge, with mental cultivation and discipline.

The great majority of the early settlers, manifested their satisfaction with their residence in this wild country, by making it their homes until death. We may, at this day, wonder at the contentment of intelligent and highly cultivated minds, so much to be admired, in the midst of privations, which, in this age, would be considered as beyond endurance, by any who could withdraw themselves from them, and obtain a residence, where there were more comforts, and social enjoyments.

The occupation of almost all, was agriculture; their taste rural; like their friends of the Kittochtinny valley, they had no partiality for towns and villages, which, when established, it was only in compliance with some special necessity, and the public wanted the accommodation. Westmoreland county was organized in 1773, embracing all south western Pennsylvania. The place appointed for holding of its Courts, and county Offices, was Hanna's town, a small village, and the only one in the district. It was situated on the old Forbes army road, distant but a few miles from the present town of Greensburg, afterwards located there. Hanna's town consisted of about thirty log houses and cabins, including a log Court House and Jail. The Courts for this large district, were only held at this place, and before Justices of the Peace. This was at a time when Virginia claimed this village, as well as nearly all Westmoreland county, as being her territory ; and in maintenance of her jurisdiction and authority, had established her Courts at a place, south a few miles, of where the town of Washington is located, and also where Brownsville now is, in the county of Fayette. There were at this period, but a few log cabins or dwellings adjacent to Fort Pitt. The conflict between these territorial claims of the two governments, were harassing to the settlers under Pennsylvania, who, as well as the officers, and magistrates, under its government, were subjected to frequent arrest, and imprisonment, by persons under the authority and command of Dunmore, the abitrary Governor of Virginia. These conflicts were kept up for some years, and even after the commencement of the Revolutionary war, and until the royal Governor of Virginia, preferring to retain his rank, and the royal service, to a republican government, fled as a fugitive from Virginia, to the shelter of the army of his King. This conflict of jurisdiction, and of the officers of the law, were, after this, in a great measure, suspended in the district, by mutual forbearance and accommodation. The title to lands was uncertain, and embarassing to the settlers, and to those who were desirous of purchasing, or making an appropriation under the government, until the boundary line was permanently established in 1784, by which Pennsylvania jurisdiction and right were quieted, and confirmed, over this large district of fertile and valuable country.

The settlers were for many years during the Revolution, and for a long time after, exposed to Indian invasions, alarming ravages, and massacres, and for the defence of themselves and families, against the savage enemy, the government made little provision, and left them, in a great measure, to their own resources.

Their means of conveyance and transportation, from the eastern settlements and markets, were the pack horse, by the traders' paths, across mountain ranges of great extent, not admitting of wheel carriages. Their trade to New Orleans, was tedious and perilous, for many hundred miles, through a hostile Indian country, and their return from New Orleans was either by sea, to the Atlantic cities, or by traversing the western wilderness for two thousand miles.

Their merchandize, and groceries, with iron and salt, were brought across the mountains on pack horses, from Chambersburg, Hagerstown, or Winchester. The first wagon that passed over this barrier of mountain ranges, to these western settlements, was in 1789, from Hagerstown to Brownsville. It was drawn by four horses, carrying two thousand pounds, and was near a month on the road, of about one hundred and thirty miles.

The first newspaper published west of the Allegheny mountains, was the "Pittsburg Gazette," in 1786, by John Scull and Joseph Hall. At that time there was no mail to the district; all correspondence was carried on by special express, or casual travellers and traders. In the fall of 1786, the first post was established from Philadelphia to Pittsburg, and one from Virginia, to meet the other at Bedford.

The county of Washington was not organized until 1781, and the town of Washington within it, laid out in 1782, at a place known as an Indian village, called Catfish, from the name of its Indian Chief, who had resided there at an early day.

The town of Pittsburg, was laid out in 1784, by agents of the old Proprietary family, on a reserved manor; yet its inhabitants had to attend their Courts at Greensburg, until 1788, when Allegheny county was erected.

In 1786, Pittsburg contained but thirty six log houses, one stone, and one frame house, and in it there were five small stores.

Hanna's town, the principal and only town in the district, was attacked by the Indians, in 1782, captured and burned, with its log Court House, Offices and Jail. Its inhabitants having taken shelter in the adjacent stockade fort, escaped the fury of the savages, through the stratagem, bravery and management of a few settlers sheltered in it, and who were practised in Indian warfare.

Merchandize and groceries were obtained for family use, from merchants, established in various parts of the country, who obtained their supplies from the eastern cities and towns, through the traders and carriers by pack horses.

It is matter of history, that the paper on which the "Pittsburg Gazette" was printed, was brought on pack horses for some years from Chambersburg, where it was manufactured; and that in 1792, the publishers, not receiving their expected supply by the pack horse carrier, who reported, "No paper finished," Mr. Scull *borrowed* from the keepers of the public stores, *three reams*, for a number of his paper, until the pack horses would again return from Chambersburg.

Fayette county, was organized in 1783, yet Uniontown, which consisted of a few log buildings, did not improve much until after 1796. The transportation of merchandize across the mountains, and the necessary articles of iron and salt, continued by pack horses, until near the close of the last century. As late as 1796, at Chambersburg, pack horses were loaded with various articles for the west, including bar iron. In that year, the first paper mill, west of the mountains, was erected at Brownsville, and until it was in operation, the paper mill at Chambersburg supplied the entire west with paper, including Kentucky.

The first stage coach was established from Chambersburg to Pittsburg, in 1804, over a rough and narrow mountain road, opened a little by the townships, with the aid of contributions from some citizens of public spirit, on or near the line. The turnpike roads, from the east sids of the mountains to Pittsburg and Brownsville, were constructed for public use about 1820.

With all the disadvantages and privations enumerated, the western district filled up rapidly, with industrious, enterprising, resolute and intelligent inhabitants, who were not deterred by such obstacles, and who were willing to risk their fortunes in this land of promise, though forbidding, in many respects.

The predominant element of character in the population of this western district, was that of Scotch Irish origin. The great mass of it was of Irish and Scotch nativity, or descent. The influence, peculiarities, and policy of that race were manifested in the progress, improvements, and institutions of the community, spread over this wide district. In habits, taste, religious and moral character, political sentiments, and social condition, they resembled much the same race that peopled the Kittochtinny or Cumberland valley of Pennsylvania.

Like it, they were still more remote from the offices, attention, supervision or provision of the State government. Their patriotism was exhibited as early as 16th May, 1775, at a public meeting of the inhabitants of Westmoreland county, convened at Hanna's town, in which they denounced the British ministry as wicked, and the Parliament corrupt, and the acts agninst Massachusetts Bay, as a system "of tyranny and oppression, and that they were ready to oppose it with their lives and fortunes."* British policy and cruelty having instigated the savages on our western frontier, to renew their hostilities on the frontier settlements, compelled all the men of Westmoreland, fit for military service, to remain near their homes, to defend the country, during the Revolutionary war, against the incursions of the many tribes of Indians that dwelled and roamed between the Ohio and Allegheny waters and the Lakes.

In that defence, they were exercised by frequent alarms from the savages, who frequently stole their way, unobserved into the settlements, surprising families, and marking their way with fire and bloodshed. After Independence, children were often carried off captive to Detroit, still in possession of the British, contrary to treaty, where they were permitted to be sold. After their depredations, the Indians, in their accustomed warfare, made a hasty retreat by their byways across the Ohio. The continued state of alarm, and great insecurity of the families of the settlers, induced the erection of stockade forts and block houses, for shelter and defence. The men had their firearms always ready for use, and generally in their hands or at their sides, in their occupations in or near their farms and dwellings.

The State government, or the Confederation, were not in condition to afford the necessary relief or protection. The obligations of the whole country and the State and National governments was great, to the brave and resolute men, who, in the midst of many alarms and perils, to their lives and that of their families, defended that frontier, against the incursions of powerful tribes of savages, and in so doing, relieved the settlements east of the mountains, from the murderous attacks of this terrible enemy. For this interposition and defence, these men received no adequate requital, either in land or in money. These harassing wars of the Indians, were continued until

* Amer. Archives, 4th Series, Vol. 2, page 615.

Wayne's victory, in 1794, which subdued the Indians, and gave security and permanent peace to the settlements.

Yet, with privations, sacrifices and trials, so many and great, this western district increased rapidly in population, improvement, and resources. The great majority of the people were contented and reconciled to the country they had selected for their abode. The great instrumentality in the improvement of this increasing and wide spread community, in religious, moral, intellectual and social condition, were the Presbyterian ministers, who have been referred to, as the great pioneers in extending religious influence and congregational organizations for Christian worship, and in extending and diffusing education.

The youth were educated at home, in the rudiments of knowledge, under parental instruction, and trained to obedience and subordination, as the unbending law of the family. They learned there the great truths of the Gospel, and "what man was to believe concerning God, and what duty God requires of man." The schools established by Presbyterian ministers, in which they were instructors, as well as the principal; or which were under their supervision, confirmed and extended the home education. The scholars of these schools were desirous of improving their minds, adding, by application, to their knowledge, and profiting under all the facilities and means they enjoyed, for their instruction. The habits of obedience and subordination that were established at home, were brought into the school room, in all their force.

The pastors of congregations, or the missionaries of the Church, by their influence and knowledge, coöperated in the great work of religious and moral instruction, by their teachings and exhortations, which were regarded with reverence, as those of learned and pious men, commissioned by the courts of the Presbyterian Church.

The impress of such instrumentalities, was not only manifested in the families of church members, but by association and influence extended beyond the pale of organized congregations; and their tendency was to reform, and elevate public sentiment, and morals, as well as the habits and manners of the people. The great success of the ministers, in the early history of this new country, is evidence of the Divine blessing and sanction, which accompanied and impressed their labors.

The old Redstone Presbytery, in 1781, embraced within its bounds, old Westmoreland, as called, which then included all southwestern Pennsylvania. There were then in it but four Presbyterian ministers. Such has been the increase of Presbyterian influence and organization, that by the census of 1850, there is reported in this district of the Presbyterian Church, in all its branches, 204 churches.*

As has been stated, classical schools were early established by the founders of the Redstone Presbytery, at Canonsburg, Washington and some other places. These, under the patronage of the Presbyterian ministers, and Scotch Irish settlers of the district, were elevated to the Colleges of Washington and Jefferson. Jefferson College, at Canonsburg, has been eminently useful in extending education in the great west. Its graduates have held a high place in the ministry, and in the professions of law and medicine, and it has given a superior education to many respectable citizens of various occupations. Jefferson College has educated nearly six hundred young men for the ministry, during fifty-three years of existence, of whom it is said, thirty-five have entered the foreign field.

Washington College has also been instrumental in giving to the country a number of graduates of distinction and usefulness. Both these Institutions have been under Presbyterian influence and direction.

There was established, many years since, a Theological Seminary at Canonsburg, under the direction of the Associate Presbyterian Church, and it is still maintained.

At Pittsburg there was established something more than thirty years since, the Western University of Pennsylvania, which has graduated a large number of students, a great proportion of whom devoted themselves to the ministry of the Gospel, in one or other branch of the Presbyterian Church. About the same time, was established in Allegheny city, the

* Allegheny 69, Washington 48, Westmoreland 29, Fayette 19, Green 10, Indiana 29.

Western Theological Seminary of the Presbyterian Church, founded by its General Assembly, and under its care and direction. It has a faculty of able and learned Professors. About the same time the Theological Seminary of the Associate Reformed Church, and also the Allegheny Theological Institute of the Reformed Presbyterian Church, were established in Allegheny city, being Presbyterian Institutions. These have been under the direction of men distinguished as Theologians, and the purposes of the Institutions were to prepare, by education, candidates for the ministry, in their several ecclesiastical associations, in such manner as would qualify them for the important office of ministers of the Gospel.

In other counties within this district, have been established Academies, furnishing a classical education to those of the county that were desirous of it.

It is believed that this rural district of Pennsylvania, under the workings of its Scotch Irish element, will compare with any rural district of the Union, in the advancement of religious institutions and Christian instruction, and in intellectual and moral education, internal improvement, social order, good morals, public spirit and patriotism.

Mr. Day, in his Collections, speaking of Washington county, says: "That the citizens, generally descendants of the Scotch Irish, are noted as an orderly, well educated, and church going people; and the best evidence of this, is the number and flourishing state of the colleges, seminaries, and benevolent institutions of the town and its vicinity."* This commendation is from a descendant of the Puritans, who, in his historic work, as before referred to, has exhibited no partiality for the Scotch Irish race of Pennsylvania.

In the early history of this district of Pennsylvania, there is a dark side not to be overlooked. That great political and moral offence committed by a large portion of their people, against the peace, laws and government of the United States, in the years 1792, 3, and 4, by an organized opposition, in resistance of those laws, imposing a tax on distillation of whiskey,

* Day's Hist. Col., 664.

known as the western insurrection, or whiskey war, was too notorious and reprehensible to be allowed to pass into oblivion. The combinations in the counties of Washington and Allegheny, were large and influential, to obstruct the execution of the laws, in doing which, violent acts were perpetrated against the persons and property of the officers of the national government. The opposition commenced with the avowed purpose of having repealed, by Congress, this law, as inexpedient, impolitic, unequal and oppressive in its operation, and especially obnoxious to the people of this district. Yet this was not enough to satisfy the views and designs of some unprincipled and ambitious leaders, who sought a prominence and distinction in public favor, by availing themselves of the hostility with the western people to this particular law, and excited the prejudices of the people against the national government, its measures, and the party who administered it, at the head of which government was then the father of his country.

That they might be elevated to power and rule, these demagogues were willing to involve the country in a civil war, and pull down the pillars of the Republic. The tendency of their measures was to subvert the government. Though they advocated in some of their public meetings, military organization and resort to arms, yet, fortunately for the public peace, there were in those meetings, some more judicious and honest men, who had not cast off their patriotism and allegiance, were not ready for "treason or rebellion," and had influence sufficient to restrain the people from giving support to the violent and treasonable measures of profligate leaders.

Congress had amended the laws complained of, so as to make them as little objectionable as was allowable to be effective, and the administration had exhausted all its means of conciliation with the insurgents, without success. The civil authority was found totally incompetent to execute the laws, and maintain the public peace. There was no alternative left to the Executive government, but a choice between submission to lawless combinations against the government and laws, or to execute the laws passed by the Representatives of the people, in conformity to the Constitution, with all the powers confided to the Chief Magistrate of the Republic.

The National government, under the Federal constitution, was then in its infancy: an experiment on trial; but fortunately for the country, at such a crisis, Washington was at the head of the government. Whilst the President took measures to call out the militia to suppress the insurrection, he expressed his deep regret at the occasion, but with the most solemn conviction, that the essential interests of the Union demanded it, that the very existence of the government and the fundamental principles of social order were involved in the issue, the insurgents were, by proclamation, required to disperse, and retire to their respective homes.

The President, though firm and decided to execute the laws and maintain the government, made, in the midst of preparation for military organization, a peaceful effort to bring the disaffected, to a sense of their duty, appointing three commissioners of talents and integrity, to repair to the scene of insurrection, and confer with them, promising amnesty, in case of submission to the laws. In this they were unsuccessful, and the President was under the painful necessity of putting the military force in motion.

It is not within our proposed limits, or purpose, to give a detail of the movements of the insurgents, or the military operations that became necessary. When the alternative was imposed on Washington, as President, of executing the law, and maintaining the government, he was as firm and decided, as he had before been mild and conciliating. His call for a military force, adequate to the occasion, was cheerfully, as well as promptly obeyed by the people. By his wise and energetic measures, and the presence of his person, with the army of citizen soldiers, of all classes and occupations, this formidable insurrection was suppressed without bloodshed, and the laws and government maintained. Bradford, the prominent agitator and leader, made his escape, as a fugitive from justice, into the Spanish dominions. Two other of the principal insurgents, Philip Vegol and John Mitchell, were tried for treason and found guilty, but afterwards pardoned by the President.

President Washington, in his speech to Congress, remarked, that the promptitude, with which his call for support from his fellow citizens had been obeyed, demonstrated, that they understood the true principles of government and liberty, and "that, notwithstanding all the devices which have been used to sway them from their interest and duty, they are now as ready to maintain the authority of the laws against licentious invasions, as they were to defend their rights against usurpation."

In the extenuation of the great public offence committed in this district, regard must be had to the condition of the country, and the circumstances of the people, at the time. They had, during the Revolutionary war, and for many years after, been left, in a great measure, defenceless, by both National and State governments, which had been disabled by embarassments arising out of the war, to afford the aid required by this isolated and exposed district. Nothing had been done to improve the means of communication, or transportation to the eastern markets. As agriculturists, they could not carry their grain entire to market on their pack horses; and because it could not be transported to New Orleans, but with great danger, delay, and uncertainty, they were driven to the necessity of reducing the products of their farms, to the most portable size by distillation. Yet they were not an intemperate people. Intemperance was not the vice of those times, we are assured by Dr. Smith, in his history of the Redstone Presbytery.* "The opposition to the law, imposing duties on distillation, was not chargeable to any special fondness, with the people, for the intemperate use of whiskey. It was the result of a delusion, respecting their rights, and an impression that they were wrongfully and oppressively taxed in the very article, which alone they could turn to account in trade, and commerce, and thereby secure for themselves and families, the very necessaries of life." This delusion was fomented and encouraged by their ambitious and profligate leaders, who used it to excite the people against all the measures of the National government, and although the mass of the people who were disaffected, never dreamed of carrying their opposition to the measures of government to forcible resistance, yet many, by attending their

* Old Redstone, 252.

unlawful assemblies, aided to create a tumultuous and treasonable movement, which they could not afterwards repress, or allay, as they desired. With the leaders, it was practical nullification, under their organization, for resistance to the execution of the law, by violence to, and personal abuse of its officers. The abuse by these leaders and their partizan confederates, of all who advised moderate measures for redress, under the constitution, intimidated many orderly and law abiding citizens, from an expression of their opinions.

In the midst of this great excitement and delusion, there was not, in any public meeting, a leader so bold as to threaten *disunion*, or suggest it, as desirable or possible. They were well aware, that the public virtue and patriotism of the country, would recoil from any decided approach to it; and that the man who would be so base and unfaithful to his country, as to propose it, would be made to sink under the weight of public odium, and if thereafter notorious, it would be by the finger of public scorn, directed to him. In those days no one undertook to calculate the value of the Union. It was esteemed priceless. It was reserved for the small politicians and noisy demagogues of these days of boasted progress, to seek elevation and influence in communities disaffected with some legislation, to talk of and threaten in public assemblies, dissolution of the union, with as much flippancy, presumption and indifference, as they would talk of dissolving some petty partnership of their own formation. Public virtue and patriotism would seem to be on the wane in our experimental republic, when such sentiments are tolerated without a general burst of indignation.

It is stated by Dr. Smith, in his remarks on that disreputable public movement in opposition to the government, that few of the Presbyterians joined in the movement, and that all their ministers opposed it strenuously and successfully.

Mr. Findlay, who was somewhat implicated, in some of the first movements of these unlawful assemblies, states, in reference to a public meeting at Couche's Fort, " That while they were deliberating, what was to be done, the Rev. Mr. Clark, a venerable and very old clergyman, (of the Presbyterian Church) expostulated with them on the impropriety of the enterprise, and used his utmost endeavors to dissuade them from it." He has also, in his history of that insurrection, borne his testimony to "the industry of the clergy, in promoting submission to the laws," and states several instances of it.

Judge Brackenridge, who was well acquainted with the influences exciting insurrection, or dissuading it, states in his history, that "great pains were taken, particularly by the clergy, in various congregations, to restrain it. The Rev. Samuel Porter, the Rev. John McMillan, and others, had from the first, borne a decided testimony against the forcible opposition to the laws." "Previous to the day of giving the test of submission to the government, Mr. McMillan, having appointed a day for giving the sacrament of bread and wine, adjourned the celebration until it could be known who would submit, meaning to exclude those from the ordinance who should remain obstinate, and refuse this declaration of fidelity. He attended himself on the day of submission and used his immediate influence."

James Edgar, an Elder of the Presbyterian Church, and one of the Associate Judges of Washington county, distinguished for sound sense, piety and purity of character, as well as for his unpretending eloquence, addressed the assemblies of the people with great power and influence, on the side of the law, public order and submission. Dr. Carnahan, in his lecture on the whiskey insurrection, says of Mr. Edgar: "This truly great and good man, little known beyond the precincts of Washington connty, had removed to western Pennsylvania at an early period. He had a good English education; had improved his mind by reading and reflection, so that in theological and political knowledge, he was superior to many professional men. He had as clear a head, and as pure a heart, as ever fall to the lot of mortals; and he possessed an eloquence, which, although not polished, was convincing and persuasive. Yet he lived in retirement on his farm, except when the voice of his neighbors called him to serve the Church or State. He was a ruling elder in the Presbyterian Church, and one of the Associate Judges of Washington county. I recollect to have heard him at Buffalo, on Monday after a sacramental occasion, address a congregation of at least two thousand people, on the subject of the insurrection, with a clearness of argument, and solemnity of manner, and a tenderness of Christian eloquence, which reached the understanding, and penetrated the heart of every hearer. The consequence was, that very few in his neighborhood, were concerned in the lawless riots."

Judge Edgar was born in York county, Pennsylvania, in the congregation of Slate Ridge, in 1744, and removed to western Pennsylvania in 1779.

Whilst we have expressed commendation of the principles and character of the early settlers of this western district of Pennsylvania, we felt bound to notice the great criminal movement, in opposition to the laws and public authorities, as detracting much from the character of a people of religious, moral and law abiding professions. The unlawful and riotous assemblies, in their midst, with measures of violence, were not only a reproach to all who participated in them, as actors, or abetted them in any manner, but were a reflection on the community in which they were allowed, that there was not in that community sufficient religious, moral, law respecting, and patriotic influence, to have restrained the bad men, who were amongst them, in their wicked and lawless measures against the laws and public peace.

The men who were actors in the insurrectionary movements of those days, as well as those who permitted them, have, with a rare exception, been carried to their graves, with the stigma on their skirts, which half a century has not effaced. Their descendants, who are now the citizens of those counties, that were the theatre of these disorderly and criminal proceedings, are an orderly and law abiding people. The deeds of their ancestors, in allowing their arms to be raised against their government, are only to be remembered to be deplored, and that all such measures, or an approach to them, shall be avoided by them, as the reproach and crime that mark, and are imputable to the enemies of the Republic.

It is a grave and important question, to be settled by politicians and statesmen, in time of tranquility, whether clemency to offenders, against the authority of the laws, and the existence of society and government, have not, in the administration of the federal government, been carried too far, for the peace and safety of the public, as well as for the authority of the laws. All those who, in times past, have raised their arms in violence, or conspired to resist by force the laws of the government and its constituted authorities, have been allowed to escape the penalties of the law for their crimes, through Executive clemency and pardon. The safety and permanence of the Republic, forbid that an ill judged benevolence shall permit such high crimes to be perpetrated with impunity. The necessity of example, for such offenders, is as requisite as it is for the lesser crimes, against the public peace and security, and if the law, in the hands of a faithful Chief Magistrate, be carried into execution against insurgents and traitors, the public peace will more rarely be violated by unlawful assemblies, and the existence of society and government not be endangered by unlawful, organized combinations of men, with their leaders, in resistance. With a known measure of punishment before them, to be executed upon all such offenders, without fear or favor, men will be more submissive to the constituted authorities and laws, passed in conformity to the constitution, and abstain from a resistance that will be subdued; whilst the offenders receive the punishment inflicted by the law. Partizans and demagogues will be as little disposed then to threaten rebellion, nullification and disunion, as they would be to boast, in public assemblies, of their purpose to murder their neighbors, burn their houses, or pick their pockets.

The western insurrection, and other unlawful combinations in Pennsylvania, to oppose the laws of the Union, since its formation, are a slur on its citizens and government. If our great Commonwealth is to maintain the position in the Union, which she ought to have in regard to her population and territory, it will be necessary, in all time to come, to manifest her regard for it, by repressing, with her own power and authority, every appearance, amongst her citizens, of organized combination, to resist by violence and numbers, the execution of the laws of the National and State governments.

Let the weight of the law and public authority, be laid upon it in its inception, and let a well directed public sentiment sustain the public officers, in the faithful execution of their duty, without regard to party or political associations and names. By so doing, the riotous insurgent, the wicked traitor, and turbulent demagogue, will learn that their criminal measures and designs against the government of the people, and its free institutions, will be as futile as they are infamous.

From the Scotch Irish settlements of eastern, middle, and western Pennsylvania, have emigrated, in countless numbers, intelligent, resolute, and energetic descendants of Irish and Scotch ancestors, who, for the last half century, have contributed greatly to settle, and make up the population of many western States, bordering on the Ohio and Mississippi.

They located themselves beside the descendants of the Puritans, as well as others of German origin. The communities thus formed, have been harmonious, respectable and influential, giving tone to public morals, political sentiment, social advantages, elevated education and religious organizations. The descendants of the Irish and Scotch, in whatever district they may have cast their lot and fixed their stakes, are amongst the most prominent, virtuous, religious, active, useful, industrious, and enterprising of the community. They have proved by their faith and works, that they are not of ignoble blood and descent, nor below any class of the citizens of this land, with whom they may be compared, in their principles, virtuous habits, and public usefulness, or in those of their ancestors.

Though Pennsylvania has not elevated one of her own sons to the Presidency of the United States, yet the Scotch Irish race of the Union has furnished to that Presidency three of our Presidents, and a majority of the United States Senators, since the organization of the federal government. They have also, from their ranks, in Pennsylvania, given to our Commonwealth, five of her Governors, and a majority of the men who have composed, and still compose, the Supreme and other Courts of the State.

In all stations under the National or State governments, civil or military, the men of this race, have generally been prominent, eminent, patriotic and faithful, wise, judicious, and deliberate in council, resolute, unwavering and inflexible in the discharge of duty; and when called by their country, to face the public enemy in arms, there were none more brave, fearless and intrepid.

It is hoped, that the compilers of Pennsylvania History, hereafter, in their review of the progress of improvement, in our great Commonwealth, in education, arts, science, and manufactures; in the promotion of elevated religious and Christian influence; in the establishment of seminaries of learning, and in the construction of great inland improvements for travel and transportation, will inquire into the authors and founders of these institutions, influences, and improvements, investigate their pretensions, and do justice at least to their merits and memory. Let them not presume to give point to a paragraph, by heaping on a whole race, some stale and unjust reproach from a bygone calumniator and enemy.

It behooves the men of Pennsylvania, who have State pride and emulation, and appreciate her prosperity and greatness, as well as the labors, services, and sacrifices of ancestors, who did so much to lay the foundation of that prosperity and greatness, to stand by her own men, and manifest for their memory the great reverence, which they so eminently deserve.

www.ingramcontent.com/pod-product-compliance
Lightning Source LLC
LaVergne TN
LVHW021357110826
845150LV00007B/1688

* 9 7 8 1 4 2 5 5 1 3 4 4 3 *